Ayrshire Monogr;

Global Citizens, Local Roots:
Lord Boyd Orr, Sir Alexander Fleming,
and Kilmarnock Academy

Edited by Neil Dickson

*Proceedings of a conference held in Kilmarnock Academy
on 24 September 2011
by the Ayrshire Federation of Historical Societies and the Centre for the Social
History of Health and Healthcare at Glasgow Caledonian University, with the
generous support of the Wellcome Trust and East Ayrshire Council*

Ayrshire Archaeological and Natural History Society
Ayr 2015

Acknowledgements

The help of Rhona Blincow in organising the conference at Kilmarnock Academy in 2011, and that of Val Wells in preparing the text for publication, is gratefully acknowledged. Financial support for the conference by the Wellcome Trust and East Ayrshire Council is also gratefully acknowledged.

Published by

Ayrshire Archaeological and Natural History Society
Ayr, 2015
www.aanhs.org.uk

Financial Assistance from

Kilmarnock and District Local History Group
Ayrshire Federation of Historical Societies

ISBN 978-0-9564704-3-0
Printed by
Printondemand UK

Contents

List of Illustrations

Cover photographs
Front cover (left): Lord John Boyd Orr
(University of Glasgow Archives)
Front cover (right): Sir Alexander Fleming
(Alexander Fleming Laboratory Museum)
Back cover: The staff of Kilmarnock Academy who were approximately
contemporaneous with the attendances of Boyd Orr and Fleming at the school.
Hugh Dickie, the rector, is in the centre of the second row from the rear.
(East Ayrshire Council/Leisure)

Contributors

Kevin Brown is Trust Archivist and Alexander Fleming Laboratory Museum Curator at St Mary's Hospital, Paddington. He is the author of *Penicillin Man: Alexander Fleming and the Antibiotic Revolution* (2004) and other books on the history of medicine.

Neil Dickson taught English at Kilmarnock Academy from 1977 until 2009. He is chairman of the Ayrshire Federation of Historical Societies, and has published widely on aspects of literature and history, most usually within a Scottish context. He has written the historical entries at <www.kilmarnockacademy.co.uk>.

Elaine W. McFarland is Professor of History at Glasgow Caledonian University. She is the author of a number of books and articles on modern Scottish history. She is currently working on the biography of the Ayrshire-born Great War general, Sir Aylmer Hunter-Weston of Hunterston.

Hugh Pennington was Professor of Bacteriology at Aberdeen University from 1979 to 2003. He is now Emeritus. He chaired inquiries into E. coli O157 outbreaks in central Scotland (1996–7) and South Wales (2005). Appointed CBE in 2013, he is a Fellow of the Royal Society of Edinburgh and the Academy of Medical Sciences.

Robert Pyper is Professor of Government and Public Policy and Head of the School of Social Sciences at the University of the West of Scotland. He has published widely on various aspects of British government politics and modern history.

John Stewart is Emeritus Professor of Health History at Glasgow Caledonian University and a Research Associate at the Wellcome Unit for the History of Medicine, University of Oxford. His research interests include the history of child psychiatry and British perceptions of New Zealand as a 'social laboratory' for welfare reform in the mid-twentieth century.

1

Introduction

Hugh Pennington

Kilmarnock Academy is unique in Scotland. It is the only school with two Nobel Laureate former pupils. It has done pretty well on the British—and international—scene too. In England it ranks with Manchester Central Boys High School (James Chadwick, Physics, 1935, and Robert Edwards, Physiology or Medicine, 2010). And with four fee-paying schools: The Perse (George Thomson, Physics, 1937, who did his prize-winning work in Aberdeen, and Ronald Norrish, Chemistry, 1967); King Edward School Birmingham (Maurice Wilkins, Physiology or Medicine, 1962, and John Vane, Physiology or Medicine,1982); Malvern College (Francis Aston, Chemistry, 1922, and James Meade, Economics, 1977); and Eton College (Robert Cecil, Peace, 1937, and John Gurdon, Physiology or Medicine, 2012). Eton is, of course, well known for its fees (in 2013 £10,689 per term), its fictional alumni—notably Captain Hook, James Bond, and Bertie Wooster—and for its report on John Gurdon which said 'I believe he has ideas about becoming a scientist; on his present showing this is quite ridiculous'.

Only two schools outrank it in the UK: Harrow (Lord Rayleigh, Physics, 1904; John Galsworthy, Literature, 1932; and Winston Churchill, Literature, 1953), and Westminster (Edgar Adrian, Physiology or Medicine, 1932; Andrew Huxley, Physiology or Medicine, 1963; and Richard Stone, Economics, 1984). Like Eton's view of Gurdon, Stone recounts that when he left Westminster the headmaster told his father 'he doesn't seem to be doing much good here'. Maybe this explains why Stone is not on the list of distinguished 'Old Westminsters', unlike Kim Philby, Flanders and Swann, Tony Benn, and Nick Clegg! Kilmarnock Academy's equal in Europe is the Fasori Gimnazium in Budapest (Eugene Wigner, Physics, 1983; and John Harsanyi, Economics 1994). In the USA the New York City public high schools stand out, notably the highly selective tuition-free Bronx High (one Chemistry and seven Physics Nobels).

Accepting the invitation to chair the 'Global Citizens, Local Roots' conference at the Academy in September 2011, the event that led to this publication, had particular significance for me because of personal connections. For ten years I was a governor of the Rowett Research Institute, founded by John Boyd Orr, and I was recruited into medical microbiology by Professor Ronald Hare, who had worked with Alexander Fleming at St Mary's Hospital and was one of his biographers.[1] Hare has shown, to my satisfaction, at least, that the *Penicillium* which alighted on the famous culture plate was not a 'mysterious mould from Praed Street'; it had not come from the street and it had not come through the window, which was never opened. Not only would that have been bad bacteriology, but the culture tubes of dangerous bacteria stacked on the window sill could have fallen on to the heads of passers-by in the street; and the noise of the traffic would have been too great. And a fungus specialist was working on moulds in a laboratory on the floor below, directly under Fleming's.

Ayrshire origins and Kilmarnock Academy were not the only things that Boyd Orr and Fleming had in common. After leaving the Academy, both spent four of their late teenage years in low paid routine jobs, Boyd Orr as a pupil

1 Ronald Hare, *The Birth of Penicillin* (London: George Allen and Unwin, 1970).
2 Lord Boyd Orr, *As I Recall* (London: Macgibbon and Kee, 1966).
3 Gwyn Macfarlane, *Alexander Fleming: The Man and the Myth* (Oxford: Oxford University Press, 1985).

teacher with a starting salary of £10 a year,[2] and Fleming as a clerk in a shipping line office earning ten shillings a week.[3] But when they took examinations they passed them with ease and with distinction. Early in their medical careers they both won Gold Medals for academic achievements: Fleming in 1908 for being top in the medical final examinations of London University, and Boyd Orr the Glasgow University Bellahouston medal in 1914 for his outstanding MD thesis. And both made outstanding contributions during the First World War: Boyd Orr in the field, attending the wounded under fire (MC and DSO), and Fleming, who had left the London Scottish Regiment territorials in April 1914,[4] in the laboratory investigating the bacteriology of shell and bullet wounds.

It may well be that their equally important but very different activities in the First World War reflected their personalities, which also were very different. Boyd Orr was brilliant at the application of science to policy making and politics. He knew how to influence the powers, both at home and internationally. In his autobiography he describes how he got his own way with the governing body when he was director of the Rowett:

> Donald Gunn, who had become secretary of the Rowett Institute in 1921, became a close personal friend. We went over the business before the meetings, and if we had anything big to put through affecting the whole Institute, we put it at the end of the agenda after a lot of trivial matters. Towards the end of the meeting, nearing one o'clock, everybody was keen to get away; then Mr Gunn knew at a sign from me whether to bring up the big item. I would put it forward in very general and nebulous terms, and it usually was agreed to without a discussion.

2 Lord Boyd Orr, As I Recall (London: Macgibbon and Kee, 1966).
3 Gwyn Macfarlane, Alexander Fleming: The Man and the Myth (Oxford: Oxford University Press, 1985).
4 L J. Ludovici, Fleming, Discoverer of Penicillin (London: Andrew Dakers, 1952).

Clearly, he was using with effect the principles described in 'Parkinson's Law' long before their promulgation.[5] In contrast, Hare considers Fleming to have an 'inability to express himself clearly and lucidly in either words or print. He was certainly one of the worst lecturers I have ever heard'. Instead, he was the arch developer and exponent of the micro-methods for testing blood that had been invented by Almroth Wright.[6] Hare goes on to say that they required 'little more than glass tubing, teats, microscope slides, paraffin wax, Vaseline and plasticine. Although all of us used these methods and generally invented the techniques we used, none of us got the pleasure from this that Fleming did'.

I suspect that both Boyd Orr and Fleming would be disappointed to see that in the twenty-first century, developments in their fields of interest could best be described as 'work still in progress'. But they would not be surprised. After all, Boyd Orr resigned from his directorship of the United Nations Food and Agriculture Organisation (FAO) because of its failure to deal with world hunger. Even in the UK today, when food has never been so cheap, varied and abundant, some children still come to school unfed. Probably the best work that the United Nations is doing today is through its World Food Programme. Separate from the FAO, it does not seek publicity but has played an outstanding role in preventing famine in countries like North Korea and Haiti. My guess is that Boyd Orr would approve of its work, but would be outraged that it is still needed more than sixty-five years after his appointment as the first director-general of the FAO.

5 C. Northcote Parkinson, *Parkinson's Law or the Pursuit of Progress* (London: John Murray, 1961).
6 Sir A. E. Wright, *Handbook of the Technique of the Teat and Capillary Glass Tube* (London: Constable, 1912).

Alexander Fleming was well aware of the problem of antibiotic resistance. He had detected it even before penicillin became freely available. In 1946 he counselled against its use as a panacea.[7] My guess is that if he came back today he would be disappointed—but again not surprised—to find that such unwise use has driven resistance to such a degree that some are talking about the the end of the antibiotic era being almost in sight.

So not only is it right to celebrate the lives of two Kilmarnock Academy alumni whose achievements have saved millions of lives, but we must also acknowledge that there is a big need for successors to continue working in the fields of endeavour that they started. The excellent essays that follow illuminate the work of these brilliant role models. A challenge for current Academy pupils! Read on!

---

7 Sir Alexander Fleming (ed.), *Penicillin: Its Practical Application* (London: Butterworth, 1946).

2

'a most interesting stage in its development': Kilmarnock Academy in the Nineteenth Century

Neil Dickson

> When I arrived at Kilmarnock Academy in 1886, the school was at a most interesting stage in its development though of that, of course, I knew nothing at the time.
>
> William Boyd, MS autobiography, n.d., p.35.

On the evening of 6 December 1886 Sir William Muir started an argument at the annual prize-giving of Kilmarnock Academy. Sir William was the guest of honour, and he belonged to a notable Kilmarnock family. The statue of one of his great-uncles, Sir James Shaw, stood at Kilmarnock Cross as a focal point in the town, and Sir William had spent almost forty years in India where he had become lieutenant-governor of the North-Western Provinces of the Bengal Presidency and a noted Arabist. Back in Scotland since 1885, he had been appointed principal of the University of Edinburgh[8] Now, at the prize-giving, along with the rest of the audience, he was liberally entertained by the Academy pupils' recitals on the piano and violin, their performances of various songs and hymns, and, as the *pièce de résistance*, 'The Hunting Song', which, the *Kilmarnock Standard* reported, was 'sung by male infants, dressed in red coats and armed with whips which they cracked with precocious aptitude'.[9]

---

8 For Muir's life, cf. Avril Powell, *Scottish Orientalists and India: The Muir Brothers, Religion, Education and Empire* (Woodbridge: Boydell & Brewer, 2010).

9 'Kilmarnock Academy: Distribution of Prizes', *Kilmarnock Standard* [hereafter KS], 11 Dec. 1886.

The chairman was the MP for Kilmarnock Burghs, the Scottish Liberal Party politician, Stephen Williamson.[10] In the presence of its rector, Hugh Dickie, who was fast becoming a local hero, Williamson praised the Academy for 'presenting a remarkably successful combination of elementary and secondary education', which he saw as a fulfilment of John Knox's vision of a school in every parish and a grammar school in every large town. Kilmarnock, Williamson felt, had gone further, for it had added science classes, subjects of which Knox had never dreamt. Although he was reluctant to denigrate the teaching of Latin and Greek, he did have concerns about the neglect of modern languages. His own family fortune had been made in South America, and he was worried that the superiority in the teaching of modern languages in Germany might mean that its citizens would come to dominate the market in Hispanophone countries. He was annoyed with critics of the 1872 Education Act, and told a couple of amusingly derogatory anecdotes of the inadequacies of rural and village teachers under the old system. As a result of the Act, which had provided for universal elementary education (or, as it would later be called, primary education) 'institutions like the Kilmarnock Academy', he stated, 'become thereby most important factors in the improved education of our people.'[11] Allied to a Victorian belief in progress, Williamson evidently had a politician's ability to spin his party's legislation as the perfection of the system. The Education (Scotland) Act, had been, after all, a Liberal enactment.

10 'Stephen Williamson', < http://en.wikipedia.org/wiki/Stephen_Williamson>, accessed 12 Sept. 2011.
11 Williamson sent his own son, Archibald, to Craigmount School, an Edinburgh private school: Robert G. Greenhill, 'Williamson, Archibald, first Baron Forres (1860–1931)', *Oxford Dictionary of National Biography* (Oxford: Oxford University Press, 2004) [online text]
<http://www.oxforddnb.com/view/article/48399>, accessed 12 Sept 2011.

When Sir William Muir rose to speak, he immediately took issue with Williamson. He asserted that 'our former system of education, though capable of great improvement, was an exceedingly good system, which had brought our Scotch people to a degree of education greatly superior to that attained by the English people.' He was, after all, a product of it, having been a pupil at Kilmarnock Academy from the late 1820s to 1833 from where he had proceeded to the University of Edinburgh. The argument was continued by the next speaker, J. Pollock Stevenson, the procurator fiscal for Ayrshire and clerk of the Kilmarnock School Board. Stevenson sided with Williamson, and singled out the contemporary teaching of science in Kilmarnock as the great advancement on the old system. When the chairman of the Board, the Revd John Thomson, rose to propose a vote of thanks, he too entered the dispute. Thomson was proud of what had been achieved in Kilmarnock Academy which, he said, with a preacher's love of alliteration, was 'never so popular, so prosperous, or so promising as it is at the present time.' But, Thomson went on, making most of the occasion, 'I have to say to Mr Williamson, when we have him here tonight, I do not think that the Government are doing all they ought to do for the higher education of the country.'[12] This criticism of the state of affairs nationally was echoed by others, but despite the caveat, there was evidently considerable local pride in what was being achieved in Kilmarnock and its Academy.

Sir William expanded on his concerns the following afternoon when Kilmarnock's most prominent citizens assembled to confer on him the town's highest honour, the freedom of the burgh. Sir William had been deeply involved in education in India and he had helped form a college there that bore his name.

---

12 'Distribution of Prizes', *KS*, 11 Dec. 1886.

As a result, he had a number of shrewd observations to make. When he had been appointed principal of Edinburgh University, he told his audience, he had asked the Scotch Education Department (SED) for a list of the chief Scottish schools. He was given a list of the higher-class public schools, those that were exclusively concerned with post-elementary education. There were only twenty schools on the list, and to his dismay his old school, the Academy in Kilmarnock, was not among them. In biblical language, Muir claimed he was 'jealous for the honour of my old town'. If Williamson had been concerned about opportunities in commerce, then Muir, as a notable imperialist, was concerned with opportunities within the Empire. In an impassioned plea for a proper system of secondary schools in Scotland, he went on to argue that their establishment was all the more pressing, for he had owned his own advancement to a now obsolete system of patronage, and unless the towns of Scotland could produce lads capable of advancing though open competition, the country would fall behind. He lamented the end of the older democratic tradition which had seen the sons of the gentry and the townspeople educated in the one school and at night imbibing the moral values of their own homes—a veiled criticism of boarding schools. Now those who could afford it sent their sons to England for secondary education as provision in Scotland was inadequate. Poor people, he maintained, 'have just as good a right to have their children educated in the higher standards as the wealthy.'[13]

The speeches over the evening and afternoon had exemplified some of the anxieties over the state of education in Kilmarnock that spilled over into anxieties about late-Victorian Scotland's place in the world. Pride in the tradition of Scottish

---

13 'Freedom of the Burgh to Sir William Muir', *Supplement to the K S*, 11 Dec. 1886.

education mixed with an awareness of its past and present inadequacies; pride in what was being achieved in Kilmarnock mingled with a feeling that government enablement was not what it might be. Sir William Muir had made some telling points: he was well aware that the democratic ideal had not been achieved, and that the democracy of the playground had been weakened by the withdrawal of the gentry from the rest; he knew that there had been good elementary education in Scotland; and he saw there were problems with contemporary secondary education, not least in Kilmarnock.

The formation of a new school in Kilmarnock had first been mooted at a meeting of the parish heritors convened by the Revd James McKinlay on 4 July 1806.[14] The opening years of the nineteenth century were a time of rapid change in Kilmarnock. Between 1755 and 1801 the population of the town had gone from 4,403 to 8,079, an increase of some eighty-three per cent, and the 1811 census showed there had been a further increase in population of 25.6 per cent, which meant that in the space of some fifty years the town's population had probably doubled.[15] As a result of a Parliamentary act of 1802, town commissioners had been appointed, and they had opened up two broad streets running away from the Cross: King Street in 1803 and, from two years later, Portland Street.[16] The bold thrust of the straight, new streets contrasted markedly with the crooked windings of the older ones. They were a local expression of the Scottish Enlightenment.[17]

---

14 Burns Monument Centre, East Ayrshire archives [hereafter BMC], Kilmarnock, Burgh Records, BK 1/1/3/12/1, Minute Book of the Directors of Kilmarnock Academy [hereafter MBDKA], 4 Jul. 1806.
15 Jas Gray (ed.), *Scottish Population Statistics including Webster's Analysis of Population 1755* (Edinburgh: Scottish Academic Press, 1975), p.27; *The New Statistical Account of Scotland* (Edinburgh & London: William Blackwood & Sons, 1845), p.543.
16 Rob Close and Anne Riches, *The Buildings of Scotland: Ayrshire and Arran* (New Haven and London: Yale University Press, 2012), p.416.
17 Bob Harris and Charles McKean, The Scottish Town in the Age of the Enlightenment 1740–1820 (Edinburgh: Edinburgh University Press, 2104), pp.93, 95.

It is in this context of population growth and civic improvement that the meeting of the parish heritors must be seen. Even the parish church in which the meeting was held symbolised the changes. The previous building had led in 1801 to one of the town's great disasters, when twenty-nine people had been crushed to death at its badly-designed exits. It had been torn down, and the following year had been replaced by a contemporary, building in a pared-down, neo-classical style.[18]

The heritors' meeting proceeded to consider the problems with the existing parish school buildings which were inadequate. On the one hand they were in a state of disrepair, and on the other, the greatly increased population meant they were too small. The meeting concluded 'that in these circumstances it would be unwise to think of repairing the old Schools—and that it is much better that new ones open upon a more extensive but strictly aconomical [sic] plan should be built.'[19] The conclusion is interesting in its combination of forward thinking and financial prudence—a combination that we will see recurring. The parish, or grammar, school, which dated from at least the sixteenth century,[20] was supported financially by the heritors, the local large landowners who had been from 1696 onwards legally obliged to support parish schools financially. The town, however, had established in 1727 a burgh school for English, writing and 'the commercial branches of education'—hence the name by which it was sometimes known, the English school.[21] It was envisaged that Kilmarnock's new school would unite these two establishments, the parish and burgh schools, in one building with the heritors responsible for the financial support of classical education, the role of

---

18 Ibid., pp.423–4.
19 MBDKA, 4 Jul. 1806.
20 Frank Donnelly, *The History of Kilmarnock Academy* (Darvel: Walker & Connell Ltd., 1998), p.7.
21 MBDKA, 'Report by the committee appointed by the Directors of the Kilmarnock Academy at their meeting on 25 Novr. 1851'.

the old parish schools, and the town responsible for the former burgh school subjects.[22] A body of directors was established that consisted of the heritors, which invariably meant employees acting as their representatives, members of the town council, private subscribers who had donated £5 per annum or more for the support of the school and, as *ex officio* members, two parish ministers.[23] The new school would continue the older traditions of Scottish education and the newer vocationally-oriented training. Financially it would be dependent on the support of both town and landed gentry.

By the following year the word 'Academy' was being used of the new school that was under construction.[24] The academy movement in Scotland was an attempt to teach a more modern curriculum, the first being founded at Perth in the mid-eighteenth century. Its first rector, John Mair, had already proposed 'a sort of academy' in 1727 when master of Ayr grammar school, at which 'the more useful kinds of Literature will be taught' and which would supply a College education to children 'whose parents cannot well afford to maintain them at Universities'.[25] Ayr got its Academy in 1798, and so when the directors of 'the new Academy in Kilmarnock' met on 26 November 1807, the school itself opening the following spring, it was joining the coming thing in Scottish education. The initial intention was for four teachers, but presumably the cost of this soon scaled it back to three, as the heritors only supported the traditional parochial schoolmaster and the town had to bear any additional costs. The parochial schoolmaster taught Latin and Greek classics, ancient history and geography, and rhetoric and English composition; the English teacher taught English grammar, elocution, and writing;

---

22 For Kilmarnock Academy's predecessors, see Donnelly, *Kilmarnock Academy*, pp.7–10.
23 MBDKA, 23 Apr. 1828.
24 Ibid., 25 Mar. 1807.
25 John Mair, quoted in John Strawhorn, *750 Years of A Scottish School: Ayr Academy* 1233–1983 (Ayr: Alloway Publishing, 1983), p.28.

the Arithmetic teacher gave lessons in arithmetic, bookkeeping, mensuration, algebra, modern geography and history, and he, too, taught writing; and an external teacher taught French.[26] The school was not free, and fees were an important part of the income, with courses costing from 3s. per quarter for writing for one hour per day to a guinea per quarter for subjects such as navigation, bookkeeping, and geography.[27] The new school was initially popular, and a report of 1810 noted that the parish schoolmaster, William Thomson, had in his class sixty-two pupils 'from various parts of the Country and some from abroad, from the age of 7 to 20'.[28] It soon proved too small, and shortly after it opened, a two-storied extension had to be erected.[29] The Presbyterian ministers responsible for writing in 1839 the section on Kilmarnock in *The New Statistical Account* (1845) were keen to propagandize for the democratic ideal of Scottish education, and they offered the following sweeping statement: 'The natives of Kilmarnock, in general, are fully alive to the benefits of education, and covet them above all things for their children. They struggle hard to render them scholars, and if possible great scholars.'

The school, however, was not without its problems. A drawn-out lawsuit in the 1840s to dismiss Andrew Weir, who was an innovative English teacher, for the maladministration of funds went all the way to the House of Lords. The directors won their case, but it left the school's finances in a parlous state. One other teacher whose career had a happier outcome was Thomas Lee, the mathematical and commercial master from 1843 until 1875. He also taught physics and, before school hours, he taught a class in geology and brightened his lessons with

26 MBDKA, 18 Jan. 1809.
27 Ibid, 30 Jan. 1809.
28 Ibid, 'Report to the Directors 26 February 1810'.
29 Ibid, 3 Sept. 1810.

anecdotes and blackboard drawings. On Saturdays he would take his pupils into the country for applied mathematical work. In addition, he made use of the observatory erected in Kilmarnock by his father-in-law, Thomas Morton, and taught astronomy.[30] But the division of responsibility between heritors and town remained a difficulty. When the royal commission examining the state of education in Scotland visited the Academy in 1868, it found that Lee had 'large and flourishing classes' in commercial subjects, presumably partly because most pupils left at 14 or 15 to go into 'commercial or agricultural pursuits'. However, despite the pupils belonging 'to the upper and middle classes of the community', in the previous five years only six pupils had gone to university.[31] It was noted that the buildings were 'in a very unsatisfactory condition', with worn out furniture, broken panes of glass, 'which it seemed no one's duty to replace', and in the classrooms, floors and walls were uneven and dirty. 'Altogether', it was reported, 'the place presents an appearance of dilapidation and decay.'[32] The commission concluded:

> On the whole the school was not in a satisfactory condition. We do not complain of the teaching. But there was a want of life and elasticity and system, as it seemed to us, pervading the whole school. There was little or no encouragement from without on the part of the directors or managers; and there was a total lack of liberality in maintaining the buildings and in providing salaries for the masters.[33]

30 'Death of Mr. Thomas Lee', KS, 5 Aug. 1876, p.3; BMC, Kilmarnock Academy archive [hereafter KAA], *The Goldberry* (Christmas 1910), pp.26, 32–4.
31 Thomas Harvey and A. C. Sellar, *Education Commission (Scotland) Report on the State of Education in the Burgh and Middle-Class Schools in Scotland*, Vol. II, Special Reports (Edinburgh: Her Majesty's Stationery Office, 1868), p.145.
32 Ibid., pp.143–4.
33 Ibid., p.145.

By the 1870s enthusiasm for involvement in the school's affairs also seemed to have declined in the community, and the directors' meetings by then were mainly attended by some baillies, a few of the heritors' factors, and a parish minister— in other words those whose business it was to attend or were paid to attend. The Academy had lost the bright promise of the early years of the century, and by the late 1860s it seemed tired and not a little neglected.

The 1872 Education Act instituted universal, compulsory elementary education and appointed school boards to be elected from among the ratepayers. One of its first casualties was Thomas Lee. Being used to being king in his own classroom under the collegiate system of the old Academy, he resigned, for he resented 'the idea of being ordered and pushed around by a body of illiterate shopkeepers and tradesmen'.[34] In Kilmarnock population growth had continued unabated, and by 1871 the town had 24,071 inhabitants, an increase of almost 198 per cent since 1801.[35] Kilmarnock had long since become, in the vivid phrase of one of the town's ministers, 'the Glasgow of Ayrshire'.[36] The parallel did not stop with industrialization. The town council shared in the contemporary Scottish ideal of civic improvement that has been described by one historian of its Glasgow incarnation, but in a phrase that might apply to Kilmarnock, as being 'Protestant, prosperous and progressive.'[37] It was in this spirit the Board entered into building a new Academy in Woodstock Street in Elizabethan Gothic that opened in 1876 and cost £4,500 (Fig. 1).[38] There were complaints, not unjustifiably, in the

34 Thomas Lee Smith to Robert Macintyre, quoted in R. Macintyre, 'Academy Rector, 1852–69', KS, 28 Jan. 1956.
35 *New Statistical Account*, p. 543; Gray (ed.), *Scottish Population Statistics*, p.27.
36 Revd Thomas Whitelaw, quoted in, KS, 5 Jan. 1878, p.3.
37 Bernard Aspinwall, Portable Utopias: Glasgow and the United States 1820-1920 (Aberdeen: Aberdeen University Press, 1984), p.151.
38 Archibald M'Kay, The History of Kilmarnock, 5th ed. Rev. William Findlay (Kilmarnock: The Printing Works), pp.163–4; the equivalent sum in 2103 would be £5,521,000.

Kilmarnock Standard that this was money being spent on the better-off in the community.[39] Critical educational historians have seen the further Anglicizing of Scottish education in the 1872 Act as diminishing its comprehensive aims at secondary level.[40] However, elections for the school were widely supported among those eligible, which included women, and unsurprisingly for the time, the poll was topped by the local clergymen who stood. The rudimentary proportional representation system of voting in use ensured that one of these would be Roman Catholic, and for a number of years this was the dynamic Father (later Canon) David Powers who served as the board's chairman for a while.[41]

Figure 1. Kilmarnock Academy, 1876–1898. This image appeared on *Prospectus of the Kilmarnock Academy* when the school opened in 1876 in its new building at the corner of Woodstock St and North Hamilton St. The red sandstone perimeter wall and its distinctive pillars (visible on the right of centre) can still be seen in North Hamilton St.
Used by permission of East Ayrshire Council/Leisure, Burns Monument Centre, Kilmarnock.

39 William Boyd, *Education in Ayrshire through Seven Centuries* (London: University of London Press, 1961), p.184.
40 Boyd, *Ayrshire Education*, p.183; Helen Corr, 'An Exploration into Scottish Education', in W. Hamish Fraser and R. J. Morris (eds.), *People and Society in Scotland. II. 1830–1914* (Edinburgh: John Donald, 1990), pp.295–6, 298.
41 For Canon Powers, cf. Raymond McCluskey, *St Joseph's Kilmarnock 1847–1997: A Portrait of a Parish Community* (Kilmarnock: St Joseph's Church, 1997), pp.82–4.

The collegiate system in which the rector was merely *primus inter pares* was over, and when the post became vacant the Board was looking for a dynamic individual to lead the Academy into the new era. It found its man in Hugh Dickie (1837–1910). Dickie had been born into humble circumstances. At the time of his birth his father had been an agricultural labourer in the parish of Dailly in the Girvan Valley, later rising to be a coachman.[42] He had left school at 13 and had commenced the life of a pupil-teacher in Paisley as assistant to one of his brothers. He had then spent two years at the Church of Scotland Normal Training College in Glasgow and enrolled in classes at Glasgow University, taking a London University BA in 1861, shortly after the University had opened its degrees to male students through distance learning. He was later to claim:

> Since I left school at the age of thirteen, I cannot say I have had an idle holiday. Even at that age I was engaged in helping with evening classes, and I found it necessary to use all my spare hours and play time in forwarding my own education by private study... Besides, I always found so much pleasure in my work, whether teaching or learning, that I never felt it hard to be kept at it night and day.[43]

His progress was swift. At just 21 in 1858 he had been appointed rector of Airdrie Academy, which had been on the way to extinction and where he had shown a talent for fund-raising, and then from 1862 he was subsequently rector at Girvan Grammar School, where he began teaching science, then very rare in Scotland, and from 1867 until 1876, rector of Dumbarton Burgh Academy.[44]

42 1841 Census, SCT1841/585, Dailly – Ayrshire p.3; Dickie, Hugh 1875 Statuory Deaths 585/00 0003.
43 Hugh Dickie, quoted in 'Retiral of Dr Dickie', KS, 24 Dec. 1904, p.5.
44 The biographical details are taken from: 'Retiral of Dr Dickie' , p.5; 'Death of Dr Dickie', KS, 9 Jul. 1910, p.5.

At the prize-giving of 1886 there was a young prize-winner in his first year at the Academy to whom we owe much of our knowledge of Hugh Dickie's character. William Boyd, who was in receipt of a school bursary, was the son of a journeyman pattern-maker and a servant maid.[45] Later he became a school rector himself and eventually the head of the Education Department at Glasgow University. In a manuscript autobiography written towards the end of his long life, he gave his impressions of Dickie. Boyd was an admirer, though not an uncritical one:

> At the time he was rather remote—he never smiled or showed any special interest in the individual pupils, though, as I had cause to know later from my experience, the interest was there. That he was basically kindly is evident from the fact that there was no corporal punishment in the secondary classes (12 and upwards), a very rare thing then or now in Scotland.[46]

It would seem that Dickie kept control with his tongue, for another former pupil admitted that at times his 'strictures appeared to us over stringent'.[47] He featured in the *Kilmarnock Standard* for calling the son of one of the town's ministers 'a big Hibernian gorilla', and when, rushing into his office from other duties, he caught the son of another minister playing the drums on his top hat, he gave him a well-aimed kick on the buttocks.[48] This was the man, then, who became the rector in 1876: self-made, forceful, and determined to do things his

---

45 University of Glasgow Archives, Papers of William Boyd, 1874–1962, DC 130/ William Boyd, the autobiography of William Boyd, unpublished MS, n.d., p.1.
46 Ibid., p.46.
47 'Death of Dr Dickie', p.5.
48 Boyd, autobiography, pp.46, 49.

way. Above all, he was an enthusiast for learning and knew its power to bring social advancement.

One major problem Dickie had to deal with was one of funding. As a result of the 1872 Act, the landward part of the parish had been separated from the burgh, and consequently Kilmarnock had lost a number of endowments. In addition the town was a burgh of barony, and as such the Academy was now officially to be reduced to being an elementary school, which meant that grants from the newly established SED were for the period of compulsory education from ages 5–13 only. It was not entitled to become, as Sir William Muir would discover, a higher-class school that was exclusively concerned with post-elementary work. The Academy's reputation had sunk among Ayrshire schools, and in the 1880s a number of Kilmarnock's richest citizens continued to send their children to Ayr Academy, which had not suffered so greatly in the changes.[49]

Yet the Kilmarnock School Board had ambitions that the Academy should at least be what would come to be called a higher-grade school, combining elements of elementary and secondary education, and that it might prepare pupils for university entrance. Dickie had been appointed on the understanding that the secondary element was to be self-supporting, as it was not legally permitted to supplement shortfalls in its funding through the ratepayers, who were in any case groaning under the burden of the cost of building several new board schools.[50] Parliamentary grants were available for adherence to the 'Scotch Code' that was strictly enforced by the now annual inspections.[51] Payment of such grants was by results, and application of the Code rewarded schools for their exam passes for

49 Boyd, *Education in Ayrshire*, pp.184–5; Boyd, autobiography, p.43.
50 Ayrshire Archives, CO3/10/2/130, Kilmarnock Burgh School Board Minute Book [hereafter KBSBMB], Burgh No.3, 12 Mar. 1883, pp.55–6.
51 Revd J. Armstrong, quoted in 'Retiral of Dr Dickie', p.5.

pupils over 7 years of age, and penalised for such matters as inadequate staffing or accommodation, and for poor attendance or discipline.[52] Dickie had to ensure that as much as possible could be obtained by such means, which meant the school performing well in exams and the annual inspections. There were additional grants for specific subjects, and it was by this means, for example, that astronomy continued to be taught.[53] Another important source of income remained fees from pupils. The prospectus of 1876 for the new school announced that the fees ranged from 3s. per quarter for infants to 7s. for the junior school. The senior school charged 9s. per quarter for 'the branches that complete a superior English education', with an extra 5s. for each additional subject in classical and modern languages, mathematics, bookkeeping, drawing, and science, or for 'Fancy Needlework' in 'the Department for Young Ladies'. Piano lessons were evidently only for the very rich, for they cost between 10s. and 30s. per quarter, depending on the level of proficiency.[54] At a time when an unskilled worker was paid no more than 10s. a week and a skilled one around 15s., the cost of keeping children in secondary education at a time of large families was an impossible demand on a working-class family budget.[55]

Nevertheless, in 1878 the SED had notified the Academy through the medium of the inspector's report that the fees had to remain within the limits for elementary education and should be capped at 30s. per head.[56] The effect of this can be seen in a parliamentary return of 1890, on the eve of the institution of free education for the lower Standards in elementary education, which showed that

52 T. R. Bone, *School Inspection in Scotland 1840–1966* (London: University of London Press, 1968), pp.76–7.
53 Boyd, autobiography, p.35.
54 BMC, *Prospectus of the Kilmarnock Academy* (n.pl., 1876), [p.3].
55 R. D. Anderson, Education and the Scottish People 1750–1918 (Oxford: Clarendon Press, 1995), p.126.
56 KAA, KA001, School Log Book 1876–1905 [hereafter SLB], 8 Apr. 1878, pp.14–15.

the fees ranged from 2d. per week for infants to 9d. per week for those over Standard VI (i.e. over 13).[57] The school was in the awkward position of being 'officially an Elementary School but having a Higher Department',[58] and the latter largely continued to serve the middle classes. William Boyd, whose father, when Boyd entered the Academy, earned 30s. per week, felt his parents were only able to keep him in education through his ability to come first in bursary competitions.[59] He described the parents of his schoolmates as 'the bigger shopkeepers, the small employers, the foremen and the professional classes, doctors and ministers.'[60]

As an additional source of income Dickie, looked to the South Kensington Science and Art Department, as did some other schools in Scotland. This institution had been founded as a result of the Great Exhibition held in London in 1851. One of its consequences had been the realisation that design was an important part of manufacturing, and also that the teaching of science had to be encouraged to stop the country falling behind its European competitors.[61] Through the South Kensington Department the government promoted the teaching of drawing and science, and Kilmarnock had in c.1868 formed its own School of Science and Art, mainly for evening classes, and had in 1877 erected a building for it beside the new Academy.[62] But now the Academy itself, through teaching

---

57 Mr Caldwell, *Fee Paying (Scotland) Schools* (London: Eyre and Spottiswoode, 1890), [p.2].
58 KBSBMB, p.59.
59 Boyd, autobiography, pp.3, 34 – 3 (the numbering in earlier sections of Boyd's MS is inconsistent and the latter page is numbered thus to distinguish it from others of the same number).
60 Boyd, autobiography, p.43.
61 Anderson, *Education and the Scottish People*, pp.161–3.
62 BMC, BK 1/1/2/5, Kilmarnock Town Council Minutes 1865–75, 6 May 1868, p.93; M'Kie, *History of Kilmarnock*, p.161.

drawing and science, was in receipt of awards from South Kensington.[63] Payment of the South Kensington grants was again by results, and there was a separate inspector. There were also bursaries to assist able pupils, the most important of which were the ones sponsored at £50 per annum by Major-General Sir Claude Alexander of Ballochmyle. In Dickie's first year, grants to the school had amounted to just over £300, but by the time of his retirement in 1904, although the increase was not entirely due to his fund-raising powers, they were almost £3,000.[64] In the same period, by which time he had overseen the removal of the school to a new building in 1898, he would see the school roll rise from 645 pupils to 845, a percentage increase of thirty-one per cent, with much of that increase accounted for by the secondary department.[65]

The SED regulated for two hours of elementary education a day, and in the inspector's report of 1878 the school had also been notified that instruction in any subject not included in the Code must not be given in school hours. To accommodate the South Kensington subjects, Dickie ran the science classes from 9 until 10 a.m., and then the ordinary school day began.[66] Annual exams for the science subjects were held after the school day finished, and they might go on until 10 p.m.[67] The science subjects taught under the South Kensington system included organic and inorganic chemistry, theoretical mechanics, mathematics, magnetism and electricity, geology, acoustics, light and heat, animal physiology, mining, agriculture, and hygiene. At first they were taught from a textbook, but

63 It would seem that that School of Science and Art was eventually absorbed into the Academy in 1889, though it continued to be used for evening classes as late as 1909: SLB, 29 Apr. 1889, p.125; the Technical Building (known to later generations of Academy pupils as 'the Old Tech') replaced it in 1909: M'Kie, *History of Kilmarnock*, pp.162, 163–4.
64 'Retiral of Dr Dickie', p.5.
65 SLB, 4 Oct. 1876, p.2; 15 Dec. 1904, p.293.
66 Boyd, *Education in Ayrshire*, p.186; Donnelly, *Kilmarnock Academy*, p.21.
67 E.g. SLB, 2–19 May 1887, p.109.

in 1882 a small laboratory, the first in an Ayrshire school, was constructed, and a second larger one was added in 1887 when an extension to the Academy was built, allowing just over thirty pupils to be engaged in practical experimental work.[68] In addition to the South Kensington subjects of drawing and science, the secondary subjects included English grammar and literature, Latin, Greek, French, German, arithmetic, mathematics, animal physiology, botany, geography, history, domestic-economy, and shorthand ('phonography'). Music and instruction in the piano continued to be available, and pupils were entered for a national dramatic competition, which could create problems in Presbyterian Kilmarnock as when Othello was the set text—it was 'not considered suitable for study in mixed classes'.[69]

All this activity made for long days for the staff, described by Dickie as 'twelve hours of work with but few short intervals, [that] make up the teacher's working day, at least in winter.'[70] Dickie himself taught all the advanced classes in Greek and Latin, necessary for those intending university entrance, as well as the science subjects. As it was not a higher-class school, the Academy was not allowed to enter pupils for the school-leaving certificate, instituted in 1888, and as a route into university the Kilmarnock School Board in 1878 had formed a local centre for the University of Glasgow local exams. A class was commenced, which introduced subjects such as logic into the curriculum, and again its burden fell on Dickie.[71] In May 1889, for example, he recorded in the school log book: 'From early morn a busy day—Examination in practical Chemistry began at 3.30

---

68 Cf. entries in SLB: 21 Mar. 1882, p.53; 28 Mar. 1884, p.77; 11 Feb. 1884, p.108; 26 Sept. 1887, p.111; 26 May 1889, p.126; 14 Mar. 1890, p.134.
69 SLB, 29 Jun. 1881, p.144,
70 Hugh Dickie, quoted in 'Retiral of Dr Dickie' , p.5.
71 SLB, 10 & 24 May 1878, pp.16–17.

P.M. and continued to 9.30 P.M. [*sic*]'.[72] Obtaining adequate teachers was a problem, and it was a constant complaint of the inspectors in the early years that there was too much reliance on pupil-teachers. After its advocacy by Stephen Williamson at the prize-giving in 1886, Spanish had been taught. This was only for a while, as the teacher appointed turned up smelling of alcohol each day, and his successor died in office.[73] However, the school did succeed in attracting some outstanding teachers. Two mathematics teachers who were to live in the memories of their pupils were John Kerr, a Glasgow graduate who had been a Snell Exhibitioner of Balliol College and who was appointed in 1877,[74] and David Murray, another Glasgow graduate, who taught in the school for a decade from 1885. Murray was a Kilmarnock native and another enthusiast for science who would eventually succeed Dickie as rector.[75]

Payment by results and the strict application of the Code, however, led to too much mechanical teaching, and there was undoubtedly too much reliance on cramming before one of the several sets of exams the pupils sat through which their success would earn the school income.[76] The science teaching was certainly basic,[77] and what the inspectors called 'mechanical and bookish'. Many brighter pupils probably coped, but it could be stultifying. The School Board, also, did not feel that the inspectors were sympathetic to their attempts to provide a high standard of secondary education. In 1880, for example, the inspector's report

---

72 SLB, 26 May 1889, p.126.
73 Boyd, autobiography, p.38; SLB, 4 Apr. 1894, p.172.
74 James Barr, *Lang Syne. Memoirs of the Rev. James Barr, B.D.* (Glasgow: William Machellan, 1948), p.17.
75 Boyd, autobiography, pp.46–7; SLB, 26 Oct. 1885, p. 92; ibid., 2 Dec. 1895, p.192.
76 See, for example, Boyd, autobiography, pp.35, 36.
77 Cf. British Library, Add. MS 56215, Agnes Smith, cited in Kevin Brown, *Penicillin Man: Alexander Fleming and the Antibiotic Revolution* (Stroud: Sutton, 2004), p.20 n.24; Kevin Brown, 'I wonder why it is that they make such a fuss of me?': Alexander Fleming in Historical Context', *intra*, n.9.

complained that the deficiencies in the upper school derived from 'so large a mass of elementary and secondary instruction under the same organization.'[78] Matters came to a head after a further unfavourable report in 1883. Again the inspector complained that too many classes were under pupil-teachers, as had happened in French and Latin, 'and that should not be tolerated in an Academy.' Using the traditional authority of the Lords of the Committee, the report concluded 'My Lords have ordered a deduction of 1/10th to be made in the Mixed School for faults of instruction, especially in the higher Standards.'[79] The loss of revenue was serious, and the School Board was incensed. It rejected the report, for, as its members wrote, 'the pupils of the Academy take a high place in the University prize list, the Glasgow University local examinations, and the Science and Art examinations—a place second to no provincial school—the committee cannot understand how the Inspector's report can be well founded'.[80] It maintained that Kilmarnock should be given more credit, both under its previous directors and now under the School Board, for its long struggle to provide an advanced education in the town. The note of provincial grievance is audible in its complaint:

> It is quite at variance, too, with the spirit of the times in favour of secondary education, that in Kilmarnock with no endowments for secondary education, and notwithstanding the earnest endeavours, not only of this Board, but of their predecessors in office, they should be treated by Her Majesty's Inspectors in such an illiberal way.[81]

78 SLB, 21 May 1880, p.33.
79 SLB, 3 Oct. 1883, p.71.
80 KBSBMB, pp.96–7, 10 Dec. 1883.
81 Ibid., p.97.

Despite the sense of injustice, there were undoubtedly problems in running the Academy. Dickie was so busy teaching that he had little time for supervision, and in elementary subjects supervision was nominal. The School Board tacitly admitted as much in the decision it now made, that the heads of department would inspect the work of all teachers fortnightly and record how deficiencies were to be remedied, and that the rector once a month would inspect the whole school.[82] The following year, instead of the visit by the local schools inspector, William Bathgate, the Academy was visited by a senior inspector, Dr John Kerr, a native of Dalry, who like Dickie had worked his way up through the educational system.[83] Kerr's report was much more favourable, and was approving of the new supervision regime. 'The improvement in several respects', the report stated, 'is no doubt largely due to this change.'[84] From then on the inspectors' reports remained good, possibly reaching their apogee in 1893:

> This large and important school is conducted with much tact and ability. The Rector who is ably supported by an ample and highly qualified staff is indefatigable in the work of supervision and has infused into every Department a spirit of cheerful activity and industry. The order, tone and discipline leave little to be desired, and in respect of instruction the reputation of the school is worthily maintained.[85]

It was almost certainly as a result of this report that the School Board in February 1893 'resolved to make the Higher Department a Secondary Department not in receipt of Parliamentary Grants from 1st Nov last.'[86] By this time, as the

82 SLB, 17 Dec. 1883, p.74.
83 Bone, *Inspection in Scotland*, p.43.
84 SLB, 26 Aug. 1884, p.81.
85 SLB, 13 Jan. 1893, pp.157–63.
86 SLB, 16 Jan. 1893, p.163.

parliamentary return of 1890, for example shows, just over half the attendances were made up of Standard VI pupils and above, and almost two-thirds of these were in the over Standard VI category, that is 14 and above.[87] Dickie had achieved the Board's goal of the Academy having a self-supporting secondary department.[88] The consequence was that in the 1890s, the average annual fee paid by the secondary pupils was £10.[89]

Such, then, was the school in which John Orr of Hollandgreen in Kilmaurs, son of an improvident quarrymaster, was enrolled on 11 September 1893, having previously attended West Kilbride Primary School,[90] and to which Alex. Fleming of Lochfield, in the parish of Darvel, whose guardian, his brother Hugh, was a tenant hill farmer, would be admitted a year later, on 11 August 1894, having previously attended Darvel School.[91] It was ably led, was attracting an increasingly strong team of teachers, had through local initiative effectively circumvented a number of obstructions that legislation had placed in its way, and thanks to these exigencies, was, unusually for the time in Scotland, strong in the teaching of science. The school was successful by the measure contemporary Scotland used to judge success. It was sending a small but steady stream of well-taught pupils to university—many of whom won university bursaries—which the middle classes now saw as essential for securing their professional advancement.[92] For its part, the University of Glasgow had recognised Dickie's achievement

87 Caldwell, *Fee Paying(Scotland) Schools*, [p.2].

88 The higher department of the Academy was eventually recognised as a higher-grade school in 1899: SLB, 23 Oct. 1899, p.237.

89 The higher department of the Academy was eventually recognised as a higher-grade school in 1899: SLB, 23 Oct. 1899, p.237.

90 KAA, KA043, 'McDougall's New Admission Register arranged to meet regulations of Scotch Education Department', Dated 26th March 1887', p.81.

91 Ibid., p.89.

92 RDA[nderson], 'Universities. 2.1720–1960', in Michael Lynch (ed.), *The Oxford Companion to Scottish History* (Oxford, 2001), 613i.

(according to Dickie's own account) in sending them such promising undergraduates by awarding him an honorary LLD in 1891.[93] He had become Dr Dickie.

In addition to others who would distinguish themselves in different fields, the Academy in the late nineteenth century produced several notable scientists: George Forrest (1873–1932), a pioneering plant collector; Sir Robert Dickie Watt (1881–1965), an Australian agricultural scientist; John Shaw Dunn (1883–1944), a professor of Pathology at Glasgow University; and Robert Cecil Robertson (1883–1942), a professor of Pathology and Bacteriology in China—all were Glasgow graduates (apart from Forrest), and all were products of the middle class, though most usually of its lower fringe.[94] The Academy, too, was the route into medicine at Glasgow for Fleming's older brother, Tom.[95] However, a distinction needs to be made between the institution and a person's experience of that institution on which many external factors can be operative—personal, psychological, and economic ones among them. William Boyd, for example, was perfectly satisfied with the education he had received in Kilmarnock Academy. Evidently a visual learner, he had even found the reliance on textbooks in science congenial, and in 1890 had become the school dux in mathematics. Girls, however, often did not profit from the existence of the Academy, for among them democratic deficit in contemporary Scottish education was especially marked.[96] The school roll book for the period gives the cause for many of them leaving as

93 Hugh Dickie, quoted in, 'Retiral of Dr Dickie', KS, 24 Dec. 1904, p.5; cf. SLB, 24 Apr. 1891, p.142.
94 See respectively: Brenda McLean, *George Forrest: Plant Hunter* (Woodbridge: Antique Collectors' Club, 2004); *Australian Dictionary of Biography* [online text] <http://adb.anu.edu.au/biography/watt-sir-robert-dickie-9010>, accessed 15 September 2010; 'Dr. J. Shaw Dunn', The Times, 13 June 1944; Ailsa Tanner, *My Parents: Eleanor Allen Moore and Robert Cecil Roberston* (Helensburgh: Springbank Press, 1997), pp.10–14.
95 Macfarlane, Alexander Fleming, p.9.
96 Macfarlane, Alexander Fleming, p.9.

'required at home'—on one page for 1887 it appears against twenty-seven out of fifty girls' names.[97] Two years later Dickie was lamenting about the science examinations: 'Many, especially girls have dropped out by the parents' request, as science instruction does not seem to them an essential part of education'.[98] It is in the context of such contemporary extraneous pressures that the experience of Boyd Orr and Fleming needs to be seen. Boyd Orr had won a bursary to the Academy, which helped his family's finances as his father's quarrying business was struggling. To attend the school he had to live with a tenant of his father some twenty miles from the family home. As he represents it, however, he found little attraction in the Academy:

> I found life at the quarry among the navvies and quarrymen much more interesting than walking two miles to the Academy in Kilmarnock. I was allowed to fire the engines and work the crane and mingled as I wished with the workmen who taught me to smoke, and from whom I gathered a wonderful vocabulary of swear words...
>
> My report from the Academy must have shocked my parents for I was taken home and sent again to the village school where I was soon taken on as one of the four pupil teachers.[99]

In his autobiography Boyd Orr consistently presents himself as chafing against regimentation, and temperamentally he evidently found following his own direction more exciting than sitting in a classroom. Fleming, on the other hand, was, according to a recent biographer, Gwyn Macfarlane, 'ahead of his contemporaries by at least a year, and clearly had a quick intelligence, an excellent

97 'Admission Register', p.12.
98 SLB, April 1889.
99 Lord Boyd Orr, *As I Recall* (London: MacGibbon and Kee, 1966), p.35.

memory and the urge to learn.' However, Macfarlane notes, 'he did not exert himself unduly, being fortunate enough to absorb what his new school had to offer with little apparent effort'.[100] He too was living away from home during the week when he stayed with an aunt in Kilmarnock, and eventually he left to join his brother Tom, now working as an oculist, and other family members in London in 1895. It would be there that Fleming would continue his education. Neither individual had proceeded to the more advanced years of the Academy, and would have been taught by the more junior teachers. It is not capable, apparently, of absolute proof at this remove, but it is almost certainly the case that Orr, as well as Fleming, spent only one session in the Academy.[101]

What then are we to make of the paradox that the teaching of a school, which was in the forefront of innovations in science education, had little easily ascertainable effect on the two most celebrated scientists that passed through it? Contingent factors such as family circumstances and individual temperament were partly responsible, but the times too were out of joint, for the former were a consequence of the hardships of life in Scottish society. However, that is not to say that Kilmarnock Academy had no observable effects in the lives of the two men. Belief in the democratic myth of Scottish education, either as a reality or an ideal, bound together the Kilmarnock School Board, Hugh Dickie, the speakers at the 1886 prize-giving, and—at least—Boyd Orr. Dickie had the ear of Sir Henry Craik, the imperious permanent secretary of the SED in London from 1885 until

100 Macfarlane, *Alexander Fleming*, p.16.
101 The contemporary Academy records did not record dates of leaving. The implication of the passage quoted above from Boyd Orr's *As I Recall* is that he was withdrawn after a maximum of one session. Macfarlane states Fleming went to the Academy in 1893 and left in 1895. As Fleming was actually enrolled in 1894, this means he had only one session at the Academy. However, Macfarlane's incorrect dating of Fleming's enrolment leads him to state that Fleming spent eighteen months at the Academy which gives him an extra half-session there; Kevin Brown, *Penicillin Man*, pp.19–20, gives Fleming's period of attendance accurately as1894–5; cf. Brown, "I wonder why", *intra*, n.8.

1904.[102] We might imagine that Dickie's counsels were all in favour of the expansion of secondary education that the Department gradually enabled. Boyd Orr in his autobiography frames the narrative of his tertiary education in the context of the democratic accessibility of Scottish university education for poor students.[103] 'It was a hard life,' he wrote, 'common at that time in many Scottish families who stinted themselves to get a son or daughter to the university.'[104] Traditionally in Scotland there had been several routes into university, the secondary school being only one of them.[105] Boyd Orr and Fleming were to take alternative routes, but their entrance to the Academy had indicated the destination to which they aspired.

Neither man attempted later to distance himself from the Academy, which is probably partly a testament to its contemporary reputation. Not only does Boyd Orr refer to it and his bursary in his autobiography as being among his achievements, but it turns up in every account of Fleming's life, and the ultimate source was, presumably, Fleming himself. For poor Scots, education offered opportunity, and the contemporary Victorian myth of progress, allied to the high moral tone of contemporary Presbyterianism, dictated that the world should thereby be improved. This was the civic vision of the Kilmarnock baillies, and it was the ethos that was to take Boyd Orr and Fleming to the Nobel laureateship. If by that time it had ceased to be avowedly Protestant and was a more secularised version, the ideal was still to be progressive. The families of both boys had sent

---

102 Cf. the annual trip to London, where the SED was then based, recorded in SLB, *passim*, esp., 10 June 1892, p.154; and Sir Henry Craik quoted in 'Retiral of Dr Dickie', KS, 24 Dec. 1904, p.5.
103 Cf. Boyd Orr, *As I Recall*, pp.40–1.
104 Orr, *As I Recall*, p.36.
105 R. D. Anderson, *Education and Opportunity in Victorian Scotland: Schools & Universities* (Oxford: Clarendon Press, 1983), pp.155–6.a

them over long distances to school, and for those families late-Victorian Kilmarnock Academy evidently represented a sign—a sign of opportunity and improvement. And it pointed to the way that John Orr and Alex Fleming would travel.

3

Science and Medicine in Scotland
in the First Half of the Twentieth Century

John Stewart

This paper discusses, in fairly broad terms, the state of science and medicine in Scotland in the first half of the twentieth century. The aim is thus to provide further context for the work of John Boyd Orr and Alexander Fleming—in other words, to give a sense of the intellectual and cultural background which would have helped form their attitudes, outlook, and scientific interests. On one level, much of this might seem more applicable to Boyd Orr than to Fleming since the latter did, of course, complete his education in England whereas Boyd Orr went on to take his various scientific and medical degrees at the University of Glasgow and to lead a Scottish research institute. But I would argue that even in the case of Fleming the notion of the Scottish intellectual and cultural context still has value and pertinence. Like Boyd Orr, Fleming's early teachers, including those he encountered at Kilmarnock Academy, would almost certainly have been educated in Scottish universities and training colleges, and, as is discussed later, Scotland in the period under consideration was a net exporter of doctors, some of whom ended up in the London university system in which Fleming himself was trained. So for these and other reasons it seems likely that both our subjects would have been more than aware of what was often self-consciously portrayed at the time as a distinctively Scottish contribution to science, medicine, and medical education.

First of all, I make some general comments about the state of medical science in the period under consideration; second, in so doing, Scottish examples are utilised to illustrate the more general points; and then, finally, I say something about medicine and the Scottish universities.[106] To begin, then, what can we say about medical science around the beginning of the twentieth century? In fact, this was, for a number of reasons, a period of considerable significance. When we think of medicine and medical science in the fifty or so years leading up to 1900, one of the key features is the so-called public health movement. In the course of the industrial revolution, during the late eighteenth and nineteenth centuries, towns and cities had grown with astonishing rapidity. So, for example, between 1750 and 1821 the population of Glasgow had risen from 31,700 to 147,000, that of Paisley from 6,800 to 47,000, and that of Kilmarnock from 4,400 to 12,700.[107] This had resulted in severe environmental problems, not least in terms of housing and overcrowding, and hence in extremely high death and sickness rates— mortality and morbidity rates—so that, for instance, a Scottish male child born around mid-century would have a life expectancy of just forty years (by the early twenty-first century this had risen to seventy-three years). The infant mortality rate for the same chronological points was 127 and 6.[108]

What happened in the latter part of the nineteenth century was that it increasingly came to be realised that some of the major killer diseases, one of the most deadly and devastating of which was cholera, were transmitted not as had been previously thought through the atmosphere—this is what is called miasma

106 For a further discussion of some of these issues see J. Stewart, 'Sickness and Health', in L. Abrams and C. Brown (eds.), *A History of Everyday Life in Twentieth-Century Scotland* (Edinburgh, 2010). For aspects of Scottish health and health politics in the run up to the National Health Service, see J. Jenkinson, *Scotland's Health, 1919–1948* (Bern, 2002); and G. MacLachlan (ed.), *Improving the Common Weal: Aspects of Scottish Health Services, 1900–1948* (Edinburgh, 1987). The longer historical context is supplied by H. Dingwall, *A History of Scottish Medicine* (Edinburgh, 2003); and D. Hamilton, *The Healers: A History of Medicine in Scotland* (Edinburgh, 1981).
107 T. M. Devine, *The Scottish Nation, 1700–2000* (Harmondsworth, 1999), pp.156–7.
108 Stewart, 'Sickness and Health', p.231. The infant mortality rate is the number of deaths of children under one-year of age per thousand live births.

theory—but rather by way of micro-organisms carried in water. The idea of micro-organisms is very important, and we will presently return to this topic. But to remain with water: obviously what were required were the safe disposal of waste and the provision of clean water for cooking and drinking. Hence, of course, the great public health engineering projects of the latter half of the nineteenth century, a famous example being the conversion of Loch Katrine into a reservoir to supply the population of Glasgow with clean, uncontaminated water.[109] The public health movement, which was a form of preventive medicine dealing with whole populations, was highly effective: if we compare life expectancy in 1900 to that given above for mid-century, it had increased for both men and women by around five years, although infant mortality was going to remain problematic for another couple of decades while, nonetheless, in the long term being on a downward trend.[110] More generally, and most importantly, overall mortality and morbidity rates began to decline and water-borne diseases such as cholera were effectively eliminated. In a sense the public health movement was a victim of its own success in that a major preoccupation of twentieth-century medicine came to be diseases which affected the individual rather than part or whole populations, although this will be qualified below. The demise of water-borne killers such as cholera, though, meant that what was emerging was the twentieth (and twenty-first) century phenomenon of the prevalence of conditions such as cancer and heart disease as the major causes of death.

109 For a short introduction to public health, and further reading, see K. Waddington, *An Introduction to the Social History of Medicine: Europe since 1500* (London, 2011), Ch.12. As it pertained to Scotland, S. Wilson, 'The Public Health Services', in MacLachlan (ed), *Improving the Common Weal*. For a brief account of the Loch Katrine project, see I. Maver, *Glasgow* (Edinburgh, 2000), pp.91–2.
110 Stewart, 'Sickness and Health', p.131; C. Brown, 'Charting Everyday Experience', in Abrams and Brown (eds.), *Everyday Life in Twentieth Century-Scotland*, p.30, figure 1.8.

But we now return to those micro-organisms mentioned earlier. Because at the same time as public health was making such an impact on living conditions, and as the predominant causes of death came to be diseases such as cancer, a revolution in medical science was taking place. For what was happening was that in scientific laboratories more and more micro-organisms associated with the production of ill-health were being identified, classified, and analysed. This 'laboratory revolution' is seen as marking the beginnings of the rise of what is generally called biomedicine, that is, the search for the causes of ill-health in, most especially, the malignant influence of hostile micro-organisms; and, the logical follow-on from this, the search for drugs to inhibit or destroy such micro-organisms.[111] As a sign of the times, we can take the example of Glasgow Corporation which, in 1897, set up a bacteriological laboratory. As an official publication put it, this was an acknowledgement that the identification of 'many cases of infectious disease was only possible by the new methods of that science', that is, bacteriology.[112] The effectiveness of this science is illustrated by the response to an outbreak of dysentery in Aberdeen in 1945. The matter was immediately referred to the Regional Bacteriologist who was able to pinpoint precisely the dairy from which infected milk had come.[113] The rise of biomedicine has had huge implications for the way medicine is viewed and carried out in the twentieth century and through to the present day, not least in the expectations placed on medical science and on the costs of supplying ever more sophisticated and effective drugs.

111 For the emergence of biomedicine, see W.F. Bynum, *Science and the Practice of Medicine in the Nineteenth Century* (Cambridge, 1994).
112 Corporation of the City of Glasgow, *Municipal Glasgow: Its Evolution and Enterprises* (Glasgow, 1914), p.248.
113 City of Aberdeen, *Report by the Medical Officer of Health for the Years 1940–1945* (Aberdeen, 1947), pp.3ff.

But for present purposes, let me make two particularly Scottish points. First of all, and as is probably already apparent, we need to place Alexander Fleming very much in this strand of medicine and medical science to which he was to be such a major contributor. To put it another way, his discovery of penicillin, and the consequent development of the family of drugs known as antibiotics, was a significant moment in the use of pharmaceutical products to combat disease. We might also reflect on the fact that here was a major contributor to medicine who was not a physician, who was not a surgeon, who for the most part did not deal directly with patients in any way, but rather worked in a laboratory.[114] Biomedicine was very much a laboratory science and its development in Scotland during the early part of the twentieth century was to be further encouraged by, for example, the funding provided by the American philanthropy of the Rockefeller Foundation to the University of Edinburgh.[115]

Figure 2. 'Tear Antiseptic' by J. H. Dowd, in Punch, 28 Jun. 1922, which caricatures how lysozyme, an enzyme found in human tears, was collected from 'lab boys', here assumed to be schoolboys. Lysozyme was Fleming's discovery that was a precursor of penicillin.
Used by permission of the Alexander Fleming Laboratory Museum.

114 For a history of penicillin, and Fleming's place in it, see R. Bud, *Penicillin: Triumph and Tragedy* (Oxford, 2007).
115 C. Lawrence, *Rockefeller Money, the Laboratory, and Medicine in Edinburgh, 1919–1930: New Science in an Old Country* (Rochester NY, 2005).

The second point to make here is about somebody who, very much, had direct contact with patients as well as being central to Scottish medical education. If Fleming was a Scot who headed south, Joseph Lister was an Englishman who headed north, holding university chairs in, first, Glasgow, and then Edinburgh from the mid-nineteenth century onwards. Such professorships involved not only research and academic teaching but also practical work on dedicated wards, in Lister's particular case in the Royal Infirmary in Glasgow and then that of Edinburgh.[116] Earlier on we encountered miasma theory which had put forward the idea that malignant matter was something which occurred naturally in the atmosphere. The alternative view was that such matter was transmitted through a medium such as water—the example we encountered earlier was the infectious disease, cholera—or that it was transmitted by human contact, that is, by contagion. What has to be borne in mind here was that many doctors in the mid-nineteenth century saw no particular reason to sterilise their instruments or even wash their hands before making, say, surgical intervention. Lister, though, had been influenced by what is called 'germ theory' as proposed by, famously, Louis Pasteur and Robert Koch—scientists in the vanguard of the biomedical revolution—and set in place a whole series of antiseptic procedures and practices in the hospital wards for which he was responsible with the aim of eliminating the very serious problem of infection. Advances such as this contributed to a shift in hospitals being, to put it rather crudely but not inaccurately, places where people went to die, to places where they went to be cured. And it is not exaggerating to say that Scotland was among the leaders in promoting the idea of antisepsis. Again this is something to which we shall return, but what was also important about Lister's work in this field was that he was, as part of his job, training the next

116 On the impact of Lister, and not least on medical education in Scotland, see M.A. Crowther and M.W. Dupree, *Medical Lives in the Age of Surgical Revolution* (Cambridge, 2007).

generation of doctors, and it was partly through this mechanism that practice learned in Glasgow and Edinburgh was to spread throughout the world.

But let us return to a point mentioned earlier when I suggested that public health was, by the beginning of the twentieth century, something of a victim of its own success and that it was overtaken by other forms of medicine and medical science. I also suggested that this had to be partially qualified. As is well known, Britain performed very poorly during the Boer War at the turn of the century, with around one third of those men who volunteered for Army service being rejected on health grounds. This prompted a lot of soul-searching about the supposed deterioration and degeneration of the British race and, in the much-used expression of the time, the need for improved 'national efficiency'. These were crucial issues at a time when Britain was increasingly in economic, military, and imperial competition with Germany, Japan, and the United States.[117]

Consequently, a series of official investigations was set up to examine these apparent problems, including the Interdepartmental Committee on Physical Deterioration and, in Scotland, the Royal Commission on Physical Training. While these bodies discovered that the British race was not degenerating in any meaningful way, and their policy proposals were in many respects conservative and wary of state intervention, nonetheless they also recognised that there was a problem, for example as witnessed by differences in children's heights and weights according to their social class. The Royal Commission therefore suggested the need, for instance, to balance out parental responsibility with the benefit to the nation of 'the improved moral and physical state of a large number

---

117 G. R. Searle, *The Quest for National Efficiency: A Study in British Politics and Political Thought, 1899–1914* (London, 1971).

of future citizens'.[118] Around the same time, B. S. Rowntree was carrying out a survey of the people of York. This found that a significant proportion of the population lived in poverty. Rowntree was, as his name would suggest, a member of that Yorkshire family which produced, among other things, chocolate. What this meant was that he was up-to-date in the relatively new science of nutrition, and part of his argument was that those living in the worst poverty—around ten per cent of the population—were unable to satisfy even the minimal nutritional requirements needed for their efficient functioning.[119] Taken together, these concerns in part prompted social policy initiatives such as the provision of food to needy schoolchildren—the workers, parents, and service personnel of the future.[120]

And in the Scottish and wider British context, meanwhile, there were growing concerns about diet which often revolved around the not unreasonable belief that industrialisation and urbanisation had effected profound changes in eating patterns and habits. The contrast here was between, on the one hand, and particularly with respect to Scotland, the relatively healthy and nutritious herring and oatmeal diet of the crofter; and, on the other, the processed, often contaminated, and nutritionally deficient foodstuffs consumed by those in towns and cities.

If you meld worries about the population's health as highlighted by children's height and weight; the new science of nutrition; and particular Scottish

---

118 Cited in J. Stewart, 'The Campaign for School Meals in Edwardian Scotland', in J. Lawrence and P. Starkey (eds.), *Child Welfare and Social Action in the Nineteenth and Twentieth Centuries* (Liverpool, 2001), pp.179–81.

119 On Rowntree's survey, and its significance for social investigation and research, see P. Abrams, *The Origins of British Sociology* (Chicago, 1968).

120 J. Stewart, '"This Injurious Measure": Scotland and the 1906 Education (Provision of Meals) Act', *Scottish Historical Review*, LXXVIII, 1 (1999), pp.76–94.

concerns about diet, we are, of course, heading towards the territory occupied and expanded by John Boyd Orr. In fact the title of one of Boyd Orr's most famous works, *Food, Health, and Income: Report on a Survey of Adequacy of Diet in Relation to Income* (1936), perfectly encapsulates these points. The scientific work on this survey was carried out by Boyd Orr and colleagues at the Rowett Research Institute in Aberdeen, of which Boyd Orr was the first director. Of the new scientific knowledge Boyd Orr commented that the 'rapid advance in the science of nutrition in recent years' had shown their 'profound' significance for health and physique. It was now understood, inter alia, that 'much of the ill-health which afflicts human populations can be attributed directly to deficiencies in diet'. There was also evidence that such deficiencies might be implicated in increased susceptibility to infectious diseases including one of the great scourges of the first half of the twentieth century in Scotland and throughout Britain, tuberculosis—the classic disease of poverty and overcrowding which claimed some 10,000 Scottish lives in 1900. Other factors were important too, of course. As Boyd Orr explained, as household income levels fell so too did the adequacy of nutritional intake while 'housing and other environmental conditions change'. It was now well known that the latter too, when on a downward course, impacted negatively on health outcomes. The 'social evils of slums' were so great that 'any suggestion that improvement of housing is of less importance than other social reforms is to be deprecated'.[121]

---

121 J. Boyd Orr, *Food, Health, and Income: Report on a Survey of Adequacy of Diet in Relation to Income* (London, 1936), pp.9, 45. On the broader context of diet and nutrition, see also J. Burnett, 'Glasgow Corporation and the Food of the Poor, 1918–24: A Context for John Boyd Orr', and D. J. Oddy, 'The Paradox of Diet and Health: England and Scotland in the Nineteenth and Twentieth Centuries', in A. Fenton (ed.), *Order and Disorder: The Health Implications of Eating and Drinking in the Nineteenth and Twentieth Centuries* (East Linton, 2000). For the course of tuberculosis in the first-half of the century see Brown, 'Charting Everyday Experience', pp.31–2 and figure 1.10.

The broader context here was, of course, Scotland's notoriously poor housing conditions in the first half of the twentieth century. Problems were most obvious in the towns and cities but could also be found in particular rural situations, such as Ayrshire mining villages. A Royal Commission noted in 1917, for example, that in 'many of the Ayrshire villages ... the privy accommodation was of a particularly inadequate standard', and while the local Medical Officer of Health claimed that things were improving, the Commission was clearly sceptical.[122] Rural health conditions, including poor environment, were also investigated immediately prior to the First World War, on this occasion focusing in particular on the Highlands and Islands. One outcome was the Highlands and Islands Medical Service which was, in effect, a form of state-subsidised health care provision and which thereby in some respects prefigured the National Health Service.[123] To return to the urban environment and again to cite Boyd Orr from the 1930s, he noted in yet another publication that the infant mortality rate in Glasgow was over three times that in the Norwegian capital, Oslo. Measures required to remedy such social ills included an improvement in the housing stock and the proper supply of nutritionally sound food. This would allow future families to 'live in decency' and to raise their children to 'attain their full inherited capacity for health and physical fitness'.[124] So here we have another important development in thinking about sickness and ill-health. Like biomedicine, this was firmly grounded in the latest scientific advances and it involved a fair amount of laboratory work. But it was also like public health in the sense that it looked at populations, or groups within populations, and how they contracted and spread ill-

---

122 *Report of the Royal Commission on the Housing of the Industrial Population, Rural and Urban, Cd.8731* (Edinburgh, 1917), pp.135–6.
123 See Jenkinson, *Scotland's Health*, Ch.2.
124 J. Boyd Orr, 'Scotland as It Might Be', in A. Maclehose (ed.), *The Scotland of Our Sons* (London, 1937), pp.84ff.

health, and of particular importance here were the roles of social class and of physical environment. The kind of research undertaken was also deemed to have immediate, practical applications.

To give just one instance of this, a very famous one, in his autobiography Boyd Orr recalled that in 1927 he had carried out an experiment on schoolchildren in seven Scottish urban locations and in Belfast. This involved measuring the impact of providing these children with milk, and had shown quite clearly that such provision had positive health outcomes. He persuaded the government to provide cheap or free milk to all Scottish schoolchildren and this was subsequently extended to those in England and Wales. Boyd Orr then remarked:

> the dietary survey was extended to various areas in England. The results showed that one-third of the population of this country, including all the unemployed, were unable, after paying rent, to purchase sufficient of the more expensive health foods to give them an adequate diet.[125]

This was, of course, politically explosive, coming as it did in the midst of the economic depression of the inter-war era when millions of people were unemployed and the state appeared helpless in the face of their problems or indeed even ignorant of them. The Minister of Health for England and Wales, for example, told Boyd Orr that there was no poverty in the country. In Boyd Orr's view, furthermore, the Minister knew 'nothing about the results of the research on vitamin and protein requirements'. *Food, Health and Income* experienced similar, and predictable, official hostility on its publication.[126] Nonetheless, and as Boyd

---

125 J. Boyd Orr, *As I Recall* (London, 1966), pp.114–15.
126 Ibid., pp.115–16.

Orr himself remarked, forms of relief such as foodstuffs for schoolchildren continued to expand. The Medical Officer of Health for Glasgow, for instance, noted in 1938 that some 100,000 schoolchildren in the city received a third of a pint of milk each day.[127]

The work of scientists like Boyd Orr—and it is worth stressing that there were many other investigations of this sort in Scotland and throughout Britain in the first half of the twentieth century—thus prefigures what today we would describe as investigations into the social determinants of health which, as the name suggests, concern themselves not simply with biological matters, as in biomedicine, but also with complementary factors such as social class and physical environment. And, again, Scottish medical scientists had a leading role to play, although of course this is a double-edged sword in the sense that if Scottish health conditions had not been so poor in the first place then researchers such as Boyd Orr would have had less with which to work. There is indeed something of a health paradox in Scotland in that up to the present day world-class medical research, and more recently high levels of expenditure, sit uneasily alongside poor health outcomes. This might again suggest that broader, cultural issues are at play here.[128]

Finally, we briefly examine the status of Scottish medical education in the period under consideration. It was mentioned earlier that Scotland was an exporter of doctors in the period with which we are concerned, and this requires further elaboration. By the middle of the nineteenth century, Scotland had four medical schools attached to the universities of Edinburgh, Aberdeen, Glasgow, and St

---

127 Cited in Stewart, 'Sickness and Health', p.246.
128 Stewart, 'Sickness and Health', *passim.*

Andrews. The first three of these had been founded in the eighteenth century and so were part of, and contributors to, the great flowering of intellectual life which took place at that time, the Scottish Enlightenment.[129] Scotland also had its own Royal Colleges, elite bodies which, inter alia, shaped the content of, and controlled access to, medical education—hence the Royal College of Physicians and Surgeons of Glasgow; the Royal College of Surgeons of Edinburgh; and the Royal College of Physicians of Edinburgh.[130] It was felt, moreover, that there was a specifically Scottish form of medical education. This was deemed to be in advance of that practised in England and, thereby, more European than British, a situation reinforced by the historically close relationship between Scottish medical education and that in leading European centres, notably Leiden in the Protestant Netherlands.[131] To put it another way, Scottish medicine was part of European, and not simply British, intellectual, medical, and educational networks.

This high reputation of Scottish medical training meant, in turn, that ambitious students were attracted to the Scottish universities, and not only from Scotland itself, where they would receive up-to-date theory in the classroom as well as doing practical clinical work in prestigious hospitals such as the Glasgow Royal Infirmary. This flow of ambitious students meant that quality was kept high. But student numbers outstripped demand in Scotland itself—only something like a quarter or a third were able to get jobs in the country where they had trained—and this in turn meant that Scottish doctors and Scottish-trained doctors

129 Dingwall, *History of Scottish Medicine*, Chs 5 & 6.
130 See, for example, A. Hull and J. Geyer-Kordesch, *The Shaping of the Medical Profession: The History of the Royal College of Physicians and Surgeons of Glasgow, 1858–1999* (London, 1999); and the references in Dingwall, *History of Scottish Medicine*.
131 See the references in Dingwall, *A History of Scottish Medicine*.

migrated to others part of the United Kingdom and indeed abroad. When Fleming and Boyd Orr were growing up and then being trained, it was Scottish doctors who medically staffed the Empire which was, in the early decades of the twentieth century, at its peak. To put it another way, there was a Scottish medical diaspora, and medical schools and practice in, for instance, New Zealand owed much to Scottish training.[132]

Here is a very specific example. Yet another product of Kilmarnock Academy, a few years younger than Fleming and Boyd Orr, was Robert Cecil Robertson. Robertson studied medicine at Glasgow University, where he appears to have been an exemplary student. He served in the Royal Army Medical Corps during the First World War and was awarded the Military Cross as well as being mentioned in dispatches. After the war he married Eleanor Allen Moore, who had also attended Kilmarnock Academy, and who went on to win fame as one of the group of women artists known as the Glasgow Girls. In the early 1920s they left Scotland for Shanghai where Robert worked for the League of Nations and where he headed up the Pathology Division of one of the city's research institutes. Robertson had developed an interest in tropical medicine while in India with the army, and his work particularly focused on the prevention of epidemics. At the time of his death in 1942, during the Japanese occupation of Hong Kong, he was professor of Pathology and Bacteriology at Hong Kong University. Here, then, was someone who had engaged with the recently-evolved science of biomedicine, who was also interested in its practical application to prevent disease, and who employed his skills and knowledge away from Scotland and, in the particular case of the League of Nations, in the service of the people of Asia and the Empire.[133]

---

132 Crowther and Dupree, *Medical Lives in the Age of Surgical Revolution*, Chs 8 & 9.
133 This paragraph draws on A. Tanner, *My Parents: Eleanor Allen Moore and Robert Cecil Robertson* (Helensburgh: Springbank Press, 1997), and on information kindly supplied by Dr Neil Dickson.

Our general point about the excellence of Scottish medical training also has to be put in the broader context of Scottish higher education which was not as socially exclusive as that then prevalent in England. The so-called lad o' pairts could, at least in principle, make his way from humble beginnings into an elite profession like medicine, although recent scholarship has put serious qualifications on something which remains part of the national mythology. Nonetheless, not all prospective doctors came from professional backgrounds, and to this degree the Scottish system was more 'open' than, say, that of Oxbridge.[134] Scottish medical education was thus at once scientifically advanced, relatively meritocratic, highly regarded, and its products widely dispersed. And as one historian has recently pointed out, it may be significant that even now Scottish doctors play a disproportionately large part in bodies such as the British Medical Association and that surveys seem to show that in terms of how patients perceive doctors, they like best those with a Scottish accent.[135]

To conclude, then, what I have sought to suggest is that John Boyd Orr and Alexander Fleming did their ground-breaking medical and scientific work, in equally important, albeit in rather different fields, at a time when medicine was undergoing profound intellectual changes and when Scottish science and medicine, and medical education, was of a high and somewhat distinctive kind. So while it is absolutely the case that we need to see Fleming and Boyd Orr as global citizens, the Scottish context, with its various particularities, is very important too.

---

134 See L. Paterson, *Scottish Education in the Twentieth Century* (Edinburgh, 2003), Ch. 5 for university education in this period. On the social origins of medical students, Crowther and Dupree, *Medical Lives in the Age of Surgical Revolution*, pp.27ff.
135 Dingwall, *History of Scottish Medicine*, p.1.

4

John Boyd Orr (1880–1971):
The Ayrshire Roots of a World Citizen

Elaine W. McFarland

Our civilisation is now in the transition stage between the age of warring empires and a new age of world unity and peace.

John Boyd Orr's Nobel Lecture, 'Science and Peace'.[136]

John Boyd Orr commanded the world stage from the 1940s onwards in many guises: as a scientist, an evangelist for international cooperation, and not least as a Nobel Laureate. Even by the standards of a remarkable generation, his intellect and energy were quite extraordinary. He lived a large part of his life in the public sphere, producing a literary and scientific output that was both prodigious and wide-ranging. His Nobel Peace prize which was awarded in 1949 recognised a lifetime spent in scientific research into animal and human nutrition, as well as his role as the first director-general of the United Nations Food and Agriculture Organization.

This paper focuses on the forces embedded in his family background and early life that helped shape the later 'global citizen'. In trying to grasp the making of the man, an obvious starting point might appear to be his personal memoir, *As I Recall*, written in 1966.[137] It is a vivid and engaging text, but, like any

136 Frederick W. Haberman (ed.), *Nobel Lectures, Peace 1926–1950* (Amsterdam: Elsevier Publishing Company, 1972) vol. 2, p.416.
137 Lord Boyd Orr, *As I Recall* (London: Macgibbon and Kee, 1966).

autobiography, it has its limits as a source. Written towards the end of his life as he reflected on a long career, it is a very selective account, presenting his personal growth from the influences of his childhood as natural, inevitable and final, when in reality the process was much more complex and uneven.

An alternative and less orthodox approach is to start from some very different texts. These are some of the school prizes and textbooks that he owned as a pupil at West Kilbride Public School.[138] It is from these rather unassuming sources that we can begin to get a sense of the mental universe of a boy growing up in Ayrshire in the last decades of the nineteenth century. Three titles stand out. The first, *Children and Jesus* (1880) by E. P. Hammond, was awarded as a school prize in 1888, and belongs securely in the lachrymose school of Victorian children's literature. Its vision of heaven was morbidly eloquent on the perils of infant mortality:

> Where little children, at his feet,
> Their Tiny crowns are flinging;
> While angels on their downy wings,
> The latest born are bringing.[139]

The second, *Historical Tales for Young Protestants* [1857], by J. H. Crosse, another school prize from two years later, is an altogether more robust specimen, presenting an illustrated compendium of Protestant martyrdom, with its stated purpose: 'to fortify the minds of the young against soul-destroying error, and establishing them in those great doctrines in defence of which their forefathers

138 Rowett Institute of Nutrition and Health, University of Aberdeen: School books of John Boyd Orr, JBO 5/1–11.
139 E. P. Hammond, *Children and Jesus; or Stories to Children About Jesus* (London: S.W. Partridge, 1880), p. 87.

suffered and died'.[140] The third work in contrast has a more secular focus; A *History of the British Empire* (1882) by Edgar Sanderson was a popular school textbook of the period. Taking a 500-page gallop through over a thousand years of British history, it traces:

> ...the advance of the British Islands, from a state resembling that of our recent foes the Abyssinians, Ashantees and Zulus to their present marvellous position as the centre of an empire unequalled in history for wealth, for power, for extent, for commerce, and for goodly influence on the progress of the world to higher and better things.[141]

There is no doubt that works like these were intended to be character building. From them emerge two obvious themes that were vital in Boyd Orr's upbringing: evangelical Protestantism and Empire. While these were firmly rooted in his own personal and family background, they were also decisive in moulding the wider cultural context in which he grew up. Yet his personal development was not just a passive process. For his life experiences as a young man would challenge the received wisdom of his childhood and modify some of his most cherished beliefs, influencing his eventual career as a scientist and a reformer. Particularly significant was his first encounter with poverty—not just the urban deprivation of a major city such as Glasgow, but also the endemic hardship that characterised small-town and rural Scotland in the early twentieth century. Almost as important was his later participation in the Great War, and his bitter acquaintance with the sense of loss and failed hopes that came to colour subsequent decades in Scotland.

140 J. H. Crosse, *Historical Tales for Young Protestants* (London, [1857]), pp. i–ii.
141 E. Sanderson, *A History of the British Empire. With Numerous Pictorial Illustrations, Genealogical Tables, Maps and Plans* (London: Blackie & Son, 1882), pp.13–4.

Turning firstly to Boyd Orr's religious background, he was born in Kilmaurs in Ayrshire on 23 September 1880, the middle child of seven children.[142] He was the son of Robert C. Orr, a property owner and quarry master, and Annie Boyd, whose family background was also in quarrying. Five years later, after a business setback, his family moved to West Kilbride, where his father later became a house painter. What they lacked in financial security, the Orr family more than made up for in religious certainty. A well-educated man, his father was also a rigorous and devout member of the Free Church of Scotland, which had split from the established Church at the great Disruption of 1843. Spiritual values and religious observance truly permeated family life, and from his earliest years he was soaked in doctrines such as 'limited atonement' and 'irresistible grace', learning to debate equally complex questions of church governance, politics and sociology within the family circle. His two younger brothers became ministers, and, like them, John was originally intended for the church.

Such is the gap between our own age and the late nineteenth century, it has become a commonplace to dismiss Calvinist orthodoxy and indeed Scottish Presbyterian culture of the period as universally narrow, bigoted, and barren. It is true that for the Orr family many pastimes were off limits—Boyd Orr claimed that he had never heard dance music until he was twenty-seven years of age. [143] Yet this censorious and prohibitive streak neglects the very valuable intellectual training that his religious background also conferred upon him. Above all, the peculiar intermeshing of religion and politics which was so characteristic of Scottish church life taught him to think critically, to analyse, to construct arguments, to interpret texts, and above all to engage in debate and polemic. This

---

142 Boyd Orr, *As I Recall*, 27–8; see also Obituary, *British Journal of Nutrition* (1972), pp.27, 1, 1–5.
143 Boyd Orr , *As I Recall*, p.31.

was an excellent grounding for an international scientist, who would be engaged in controversy throughout his career.

At the age of thirteen, Boyd Orr won a bursary to Kilmarnock Academy, but he was quickly removed and returned to the village school, apparently because he was spending too much time in the dubious company of his father's quarry workers. He became a pupil-teacher at West Kilbride while also working in the family business and studying to gain university entrance qualifications. In *As I Recall*, he implies that religious doubt crept in early and that he discarded the 'old beliefs', as soon as he left home to pursue his Arts degree at Glasgow University in the late 1890s.[144] This seems a convenient over-simplification. Amongst his huge list of scientific publications, there is something of an oddity: *Scotch Church Crisis: The Full Story of the Modern Phase of the Presbyterian Struggle*, which was published in 1905, when Boyd Orr was living in Saltcoats.[145] Again, his autobiography is dismissive, hinting that this was merely a pamphlet, written as an act of filial piety. In fact, the work amounts to 121 pages of concentrated theological wrangling. The background was an extraordinary storm that tore apart Scottish Presbyterianism at the turn of the century. The union of two leading Presbyterian denominations, the Free Kirk and the United Presbyterians, in 1900 was accepted by the great majority of members. However, a tiny minority—Robert Orr among them—actively resisted the measure. Some of their concerns centred on church governance, and in particular the church-state relationship, but most importantly they distrusted the theological modernization

---

144 Boyd Orr , *As I Recall*, pp.32–3.
145 J. B. Orr, *Scotch Church Crisis: The Full Story of the Modern Phase of the Presbyterian Struggle* (Glasgow: M'Neilage, 1905). His memoirs imply that it appeared shortly after his graduation in 1902.

embraced by the new united body, the United Free Church (UFC).[146] They believed that the UFC had turned its back on biblical Christianity and deserted the tenets of pure Calvinism. The tenacious band of some twenty-seven ministers and perhaps about ninety congregations were sarcastically designated 'the Wee Frees', and in response, nine of its ministers and eleven elders took the UFC to court to seize its assets, arguing they were the true heirs of the Disruption. It was a David and Goliath struggle, but, although they lost the first round in the Court of Session, the decision was reversed on appeal by the House of Lords in August 1904.[147] As a result, the wealth of one of Scotland's biggest denominations—more than £10 million in funds, over 1000 churches and manses, as well as the Assembly Hall, theological colleges and mission stations—fell into their lap. This was an incredible judgement, but even though a subsequent parliamentary act divided the property and funds,[148] the rump of the Free Church of Scotland emerged with a generous financial settlement that would underpin its future.

Far from being a detached observer, John Boyd Orr was in the thick of the 'Scotch Church Crisis'. He set out his vision for the new church:

> But, if after all, the Divine authorship of the Bible be a reality, the Free Church has
> a great work both social and religious, compared with which the Disruption was
> a mere arrogant whim. It must stand as a rampart against infidelity, mammon
> worship, and pleasure-seeking, that is spread over all the land like a pall, and save
> our country from the scepticism and spiritual stagnation, with the accompanying

146 J. R. Fleming, *A History of the Church in Scotland, 1843–1929*, vol. 2 (Edinburgh: T. & T. Clark, 1933), pp.56–80. The situation was particularly bitter and long-lasting in West Kilbride where both parties squabbled over use of the local St Bride's Church. For Robert Orr's correspondence on the issue see: *Ardrossan and Saltcoats Herald*, 15 Jan. 1905.
147 *Bannatyne v. The United Free Church of Scotland* (1902) 4 F. 1083; *General Assembly of the Free Church of Scotland v. Lord Overtoun* (1904) 7 F. 202.
148 Churches (Scotland) Act, 1905, 5 Edward VII, c. 12.

irreligion and low standard of morality that characterised the eighteenth century. Grounded on truth, and purged of the higher critics and political jugglers, it will recuperate its strength and outlive the misrepresentation and calumny heaped on it by the impotent rage of a foiled adversary. In generations to come people will think on the fiery ordeal through which it is now passing, and read with a new meaning its motto:

'NEC TAMEN CONSUMEBATUR'[149]

These are hardly the words of a man who is writing simply to please his father. He was already developing the combative style of advocacy that would serve him well in his international career. However, there is no doubt that quite shortly after his intervention in the Free Church controversy, he did increasingly turn away from organised religion. There were various reasons for this, but one clue is contained in the passage above when he stresses the great 'social' mission of the new church.

On gaining his first degree in 1902 he had taken a job as a schoolteacher in one of Glasgow's worst slum areas. Nothing in his Ayrshire youth and boyhood had prepared him for the extent of the urban poverty that now confronted him. Free elementary education in the city had been eventually achieved in 1900 and the school leaving age was raised by the government from thirteen to fourteen the next year, but hunger, air pollution and chronic overcrowding in the home environment tended to undermine the reformers' good intentions.[150] For example, nearly one third of children admitted to Glasgow's Belvidere Fever Hospital around 1910 had visible symptoms of previous attacks of rickets, a condition

---

149 Orr, *Scotch Church Crisis*, p.103; the motto alludes to Ex. 3: 2 and translates as 'yet it was not consumed'.
150 I. Maver, *Glasgow* (Edinburgh: Edinburgh University Press, 2000), p.185.

which weakened sufferers and made them susceptible to other diseases.[151] Boyd Orr wrote of returning home from his work as a teacher feeling physically sick and depressed, as there was nothing he could do to help his pupils, many of whom were suffering from basic malnutrition.[152] Even when he moved out of the city and took up a teaching post at Kyleshill School in Saltcoats, a small elementary school with a roll of 120 pupils, he could not escape from poverty, or from the limiting effect it had on the educational horizons of the children in his care.[153] Although this typical Scottish town was a more socially-mixed community, with a growing tourist trade, its once thriving harbour was entering a period of terminal decline, and it was subject to the same pattern of cyclical depressions which plagued the Scottish economy as a whole.[154]

Against this background, Boyd Orr became concerned that the churches were more interested in their own internal politics than the challenges imposed by the world around them. In the *Scotch Church Crisis* he had already thrown out a challenge to his UFC opponents:

> What a huge organisation! What vast possibilities for work!' says the social reformer. Are you endeavouring to raise the submerged tenth, fighting against the drunkenness and sin, the squalor and diseases of the slums, snatching men from the prison gates, feeding the hungry, and finding asylum for the human derelicts that float about in our cities? The Church looks at its soft white hands and with a shudder refers him to the Salvation Army.[155]

151 T. C. Smout, *A Century of the Scottish People* (London: Fontana, 1997), pp.123–4.
152 Boyd Orr, *As I Recall*, p.44.
153 *Ardrossan and Saltcoats Herald*, 15 Mar. 1905.
154 The numbers of the poor who were chargeable to Ardrossan Parish increased steeply between 1904 and 1905: *Ardrossan and Saltcoats Herald*, 11 Aug. 1905.
155 Orr, *Scotch Church Crisis*, p.98.

He did not lose his religious faith—towards the end of his life he was drawn to the simplicity of the Quaker movement—but he began to follow a new secular gospel—the gospel of common brotherhood. He would pursue this quest for a new world order, based on freedom from want, with the same sincerity and commitment that he had once devoted to evangelical Protestantism and the Free Kirk.

Figure 3. 'Problem of our Time: From Land to Mouth' by David Low from the *Evening Standard*, 26 Aug. 1947, illustrating one of Boyd Orr's major concerns when director of the United Nations Food and Agriculture Organisation.
Used by permission of David Low/Solo Syndication and the British Cartoon Archive, University of Kent.

The second major theme in the making of John Boyd Orr—that of 'empire'—reinforced the growth of this confident, outward-looking spirit. Again, it is important to acknowledge the gulf that exists between the negative connotations of 'imperialism' in our day, and the way that empire was understood and valued in late nineteenth-century Scotland. In his Sanderson's textbook, the young Boyd Orr could read of an Empire whose area exceeded eleven million and a half square miles, and whose population had reached 420 million by the 1880s.[156] Many Scots were deeply engaged in the British imperial project. There were two important dimensions to this, both having an influence on Boyd Orr's boyhood and youth.

In the first place, Scottish soldiers were hailed as the 'bulwarks' of Empire, defending imperial territories from the North-West Frontier to the Sudan.[157] Popular militarism was hardly unique in this period across Europe, but the Scottish variant was particularly effective as a practical junction point between local patriotism, national identity, and imperial destiny. There was also an interesting local connection. The village of West Kilbride was home to two distinguished soldiers: General Sir Archibald Hunter, who won the appellation, 'Kitchener's Sword Arm', for his service in the Sudan campaign, and Aylmer Hunter-Weston of Hunterston, who would rise to become a Lieutenant-General and Corps Commander in the Great War.[158] Boyd Orr was by no means immune from the attractions of the Scottish martial tradition, and his interest in soldiering was further stimulated by the outbreak of the Second South African War in 1899.

156 Sanderson, *History of the British Empire*, pp.420–427.
157 S. Allen and A. Carswell, *The Thin Red Line. War, Empire and Visions of Scotland* (Edinburgh: National Museums of Scotland, 2004); E. Spiers, *The Scottish Soldier and Empire, 1854–1902* (Edinburgh, 2006).
158 The world of the Ayrshire gentry was a small one. The two families were not related, but were neighbours and friends: *Ardrossan and Saltcoats Herald*, 8 Dec. 1905.

These were heady days in Ayrshire and throughout Scotland, as the early reversals of the British Army led to a call for 'citizen volunteers': thousands responded by attempting to join the local yeomanry, or service battalions of Scottish infantry regiments.[159] Boyd Orr was not able to enlist on this occasion, but he remained fascinated by military life and became an enthusiastic member of the officer training corps at Glasgow University.

Yet, imperialism had another meaning in Scotland beyond military conquest. For many Scots, the British Empire was rooted in progressive values, in the ideals of 'liberty' and 'progress'.[160] Imperialism was viewed as a civilising force, a deeply 'moral' project, bringing betterment to peoples within its boundaries. This prevailing cultural climate was important in encouraging Boyd Orr to look outwards, acting as a counterpoint to that intense, introspective, and peculiarly Scottish world into which his religious upbringing could so easily have locked him. Instead, he was accustomed from the outset to think about issues on a world scale. Obviously, he moved beyond his early beliefs and he certainly did not remain a conventional imperialist, but the habit of 'thinking globally' remained. Ironically, the context of much of his work on agriculture and world hunger in the post-war period would be set by decolonisation and great-power rivalry, an era which he had hoped would have eventually ushered in a new age of cooperation and world peace. Indeed, he believed that the positive legacy of Empire had uniquely equipped Britain to lead the struggle to develop the earth's resources

159 E. W. McFarland, '"Empire-Enlarging Genius": Scottish Imperial Yeomanry Volunteers in the Boer War', *War in History*, 13/3 (July 2006), pp.299–328. For personal testimony from Ayrshire recruits, see A. S. Orr [no relation], *With the Scottish Yeomanry in South Africa 1900–1. A Record of the Work and Experiences of the Glasgow and Ayrshire Company* (Glasgow, 1901); R. McCaw, *With the Ayrshire Volunteers in South Africa* (Kilmarnock, 1901).

160 J. Kennedy, *Liberal Nationalisms: Empire, State, and Civil Society in Scotland and Quebec* (Montreal: McGill-Queen's University Press, 2013), pp. 81–118.

for the benefit of the peoples of all countries. In the acceptance speech that followed his installation as the first Honorary Burgess of Saltcoats in November 1948, he argued:

> Our great Commonwealth is far too great a power to become a satellite of either of the two new World Powers. It is a nearest approach to a community of free nations of all colours and countries which the world has ever seen. Its natural resources are greater than the USSR or USA. This country, which is at the centre of the Commonwealth, should take the lead in getting the nations to work together through the United Nations Organisation, to get trade going full blast to create a world of plenty and prosperity which is the only basis of world peace.[161]

The final set of experiences that were vital to the making of Boyd Orr, and indeed of a whole generation of Scots, were rooted in the Great War. On the eve of the outbreak of war in 1914, his career had already been through various evolutions. He knew he was not cut out for teaching, and leaving Kyleshill after three years, he returned to Glasgow University to complete a science and medicine course. On graduation in 1912, after gaining two degrees in record time, he became a ship's doctor and then briefly returned to Saltcoats to sample life as a locum GP. Neither post was lucrative enough to suit him—a constant imperative in his adult life would be the search for financial security, doubtless another product of his family background. Instead, he had taken up a new post as a research director at the embryonic research institute in animal nutrition at Aberdeen (later known as the Rowett Institute), and was busily engaged in building up its research capacity.

---

161 *Ardrossan and Saltcoats Herald*, 12 Nov. 1948.

The outbreak of war changed everything. There was a huge psychological mobilisation behind the war effort in Scotland. The keynote was defensive patriotism, with the war hailed as a just and necessary crusade against an aggressor who threatened the very survival of the British Empire.[162] Despite Boyd Orr's later commitment to 'World Peace', he was not a pacifist and felt it was his duty to enlist. He was far from alone—Scotland raised a total of 320,589 men during the period of voluntary enlistment that consisted of one in four of Scottish males between 15 and 49, and thirteen per cent of the UK total.[163] It is striking that he did not want to join up as doctor, but as an infantry officer. However, he was posted to the Royal Army Medical Corps, and went on to serve with the Sherwood Foresters all the way through the war until 1918; he then volunteered again, this time as a Royal Navy surgeon, before being seconded back to the army for a study of soldiers' dietary needs. He had an eventful war. Although supposedly a non-combatant officer, casualties in his unit at the Somme meant that he took command of a bombing platoon. He won the MC (with a later bar) at the Somme and the DSO at Passchendaele. But initially, he refused to wear his medal ribbons, partly because he believed that the 'really brave men were dead with no medals'.[164]

Scotland was mauled by the Great War. The official figure of 74,000 War Dead was almost immediately scaled up to 100,000, with the spectre of Scotland's 'hundred thousand dead' haunting the post war decades. Boyd Orr's brother, Jimmy, was numbered among them. Newly appointed as minister at Shettleston Free Church, he had enlisted in 1914 as a private. He was later commissioned as

---

162 E. W. McFarland, 'The Great War', in T. M. Devine and J. Wormald (eds.), *The Oxford Companion of Modern Scottish History* (Oxford: Oxford University Press, 2012), pp.553–568.
163 E. Spiers, 'The Scottish Soldier at War', in H. Cecil and P.H. Liddle (eds.), *Facing Armageddon. The First World War Experienced* (London: Pen & Sword, 1996), p.315.
164 Boyd Orr, *As I Recall*, p.78.

a captain in the 4th Royal Scots Fusiliers, and was killed at Passchendaele in July 1917.[165] History would repeat itself in the next war when Boyd Orr's only son 'Billy', a sergeant in the RAF, was killed in action on Christmas Day 1941, while flying on a Coastal Command mission.

As the war memorials were erected in towns and villages all over Scotland, there was a sense that the new society which emerged from the Great War must be worthy of those who had made the supreme sacrifice. The war dead were 'ideal citizens' whose sacrifice was a crucial component of victory, and one which imposed duties on survivors. Death had to be made meaningful through building a 'new' Scotland and a 'better' Britain. As General Hunter-Weston assured the congregation of Kilmaurs Parish Church in July 1922, 'the best memorial we can dedicate to their memory is the dedication for their sake and the sake of the country they died for that we will do our bit and do it cheerily, for others not ourselves'.[166] For Boyd Orr, 'doing his bit' was returning to Scotland in 1919 to manage the Rowett Institute, which he was determined to turn into a world-class research powerhouse.

Of course, the new Scotland and the better Britain did not materialise. Instead, the 1920s and 30s have been described as the 'Devil's decades', as the crisis of the world economy defeated the reconstruction of post-war Scotland, which now paid the price for its historic dependence on imperial markets.[167] The moral purpose of the immediate post-war years was replaced by a sense of waste and disappointment. Scotland's war losses became in themselves part of the

---

165 *Ardrossan and Saltcoats Herald*, 10 Aug. 1917.
166 *Kilmarnock Standard*, 10 Jul. 1922.
167 D. Newlands, 'The Regional Economies of Scotland', in T. M. Devine, C. H. Lee and G. Peden (eds.), *The Transformation of Scotland. The Economy Since 1707* (Edinburgh: Edinburgh University Press, 2005), pp.168–8.

explanation of economic decline—the death of so many junior officers, like Jimmy Orr, was believed to have robbed Scottish industry and society of their future leaders

Boyd Orr was a survivor, and any disillusionment he may have felt over post-war conditions was channelled into his scientific work and into public advocacy for a national food policy. Research at the Rowett increasingly broadened out from animal into human nutrition. Keenly aware that the basic poverty, and poor health and nutrition, he had first witnessed as a young man at the turn of the century had by no means dissipated, he pressed during the 1930s not just for national but for international action. The basis was laid for his future career as an advocate for worldwide cooperation to end poverty and malnutrition.

In conclusion, in trying to understand a towering figure like John Boyd Orr, it is very easy to view him through the prism of present-day values and concerns, even plundering his career for meaningful 'precedents'. However, this discussion has argued that to understand the making of the man, our starting point should be to place him in the context of his own times. Above all, we must grasp the complicated alchemy between the ideas and assumptions with which he grew up, and his later bitter exposure to poverty and war, that made this Ayrshireman into a true 'global citizen'.

Even when championing the new world order in his Nobel Lecture, he could not forget the old precepts of his youth:

> Let there be less talk of war, which implies fear and panic, and more of the great new age struggling to be born. Let us all work for it. Let the churches which believe in the eternal and unchangeable truth proclaimed by Jesus of Nazareth redouble their efforts for peace so that we in our day may see the beginning of the building of the new and better world which our children shall inherit.[168]

168 Haberman, *Nobel Lectures*, p.428.

5

John Boyd Orr:
Idealism, Pragmatism, and Social Justice

Robert Pyper

It would be wrong to describe John Boyd Orr as a forgotten figure. The true lost souls of history tend not to have university buildings and streets named after them, and Boyd Orr's name adorns one of the 1970s teaching blocks at the University of Glasgow and the streets of several small towns in the west of Scotland. However, given his contributions to public policy in the United Kingdom, his international impact, and considering the nature of the interests and concerns which dominated his life, it is rather odd that he generally features only as one of the characters from the footnotes of twentieth-century history. No full-scale biography of Boyd Orr has been written, and his name figures only fleetingly, at best, in current debates on matters such as public health and social exclusion, the role of the United Nations, and third-world poverty. Yet these were the concerns and preoccupations of his life, and his contribution to our understanding of these matters was significant. Although in appearance, style, and manner, Boyd Orr was a quintessential early twentieth-century figure, his work was far-sighted and should resonate in our modern world. His instincts did not fall neatly within a party framework, although he moved in political circles throughout his career, had some Scottish nationalist leanings, was, briefly, a Member of Parliament (as an Independent), and then sat in the House of Lords (as a crossbencher). The twin themes of pragmatism and idealism ran through his life, and he was a true political figure, in the broadest sense of the term.

In contemporary photographs and cartoons (including Vicky's 'cabinet of eggheads' from the *New Statesman* in 1958 (Fig. 4), which featured Boyd Orr alongside such luminaries as Bertrand Russell and T. S. Eliot),[169] he appears as an imposing figure, with a rugged face, huge nose and improbably bushy eyebrows. He has the look of an avuncular Victorian public servant, or an Old Testament prophet, albeit one with a glint of mischief in his eyes. Indeed, his life work was truly Victorian in its scope and scale.

THE NEW CABINET
"A COUNTRY NEGLECTS ITS EGGHEADS AT ITS PERIL ... IT IS TIME WE GOT TOGETHER "
- LORD HAILSHAM

Figure 4. 'The New Cabinet' by Vicky, from the *New Statesman*, 4 Jan. 1958, based on a speech by Quintin Hogg, Viscount Hailsham, to the Royal Society on 30 Nov.1957, in which he said: 'A country neglects its eggheads at its peril... It is the egghead who discovers penicillin... let us join in a united protest to Downing Street and the White House demanding higher recognition.' In Vicky's 'new cabinet', Boyd Orr appears as the minister for agriculture and is the only Scot included in the group.
From left to right (standing): Lord Boyd Orr; John Osborne; Dame Edith Sitwell; Malcolm Muggeridge; Bertrand Russell; and Capt. B. H. Liddell Hart; (seated): A. J. P. Taylor; T. S. Eliot; Viscount Hailsham; Victor Gollancz; and Kingsley Martin; (standing miniature): Vicky [i.e. Victor Weisz].
Used by permission of the British Cartoon Archive, University of Kent.

169 The cartoon was reproduced in Lord Boyd Orr, *As I Recall* (London: Macgibbon and Kee, 1966), illustrations facing p.193.

A Series of 'Lives'

The influences of John Boyd Orr's Ayrshire roots set out in Professor McFarland's paper ('evangelical Protestantism', 'Empire', and, of course, the Protestant work ethic), bore upon the continuities and contradictions of his life and work. It was a life of several parts, in many ways a series of 'lives', but running through all of these was a sense of duty and obligation, an idealism tempered by pragmatism, and a consistent commitment to social justice at home and abroad.

Lord Ritchie-Calder, the eminent Scottish journalist, author and academic, in the introduction to his friend's autobiography summarised Boyd Orr's work in terms of numerous 'aliases' by which he might be known:

> as a schoolteacher; as a distinguished medical student; as a research worker; as a soldier (M.C., D.S.O.); as a sailor; as the creator of a world-famous scientific institute; as a Fellow of the Royal Society; as an evangelist for social justice; as a farmer; as a banker; as a Member of Parliament; as the director-general of the United Nations' Food and Agriculture Organisation; as the Chancellor of Glasgow University; as a Peer of the Realm; and as a Nobel Laureate for Peace.[170]

This list covers only some of the man's activities, of course. He also lived a large part of his life as one of the 'great and the good' within that world of official and semi-official advisory committees and regulatory bodies, later described as quangos and NGOs. However, Calder was quick to acknowledge that any assessment of Boyd Orr's life based solely on the posts he occupied and the titles he held would be inadequate.

---

170 Ritchie Calder, 'Introduction. About the Man Who Wrote This Book', in Boyd Orr, *As I Recall*, p.13.

The foundations for his life's work were laid during his upbringing, teaching experiences in Ayrshire and Glasgow, student life at Glasgow University, and voluntary Christian mission work in the city. Direct encounters with poverty and its consequences for people's health and education in the years before he became medically qualified and then embarked on a career in scientific research (which was interrupted by service in the Great War) clearly marked Boyd Orr, and had a significant impact on his subsequent activities.

From these foundations he built a substantial edifice. Even by the standards of his own generation, and allowing for the driving influence of the Protestant work ethic, Boyd Orr's output was prodigious. Books, scholarly articles for academic journals, reports, popular articles for newspapers, speeches, broadcast talks, memoranda, and letters were churned out year after year. His papers, dispersed across a range of locations, including the Rowett Institute, the National Library of Scotland, the National Archives, and other libraries, shed light on the unceasing activity which stemmed from his feeling of duty (as well as from an undoubtedly strong ambition).

The Key Contributions Summarised

Inter-War Period

Following his service in the Great War, Boyd Orr returned to Aberdeen to resume the work at the Rowett Institute he had commenced just a few months before the conflict started.[171] There, he established his reputation by managing the financial, physical, and scientific development of the former 'Nutrition Institute', which was renamed in honour of John Quiller Rowett, one of its key benefactors. At an early stage, in line with his own interests, Boyd Orr secured permission for the Rowett to follow-up possible human nutritional implications stemming from any of its work on animal nutrition. This led to the studies which propelled the name of Boyd Orr, and the Rowett, into the centre of British social and public policy in the 1930s.

171 Boyd Orr's association with what became the Rowett Institute started when, having completed his degrees in science and medicine, and following brief spells as a ship's surgeon on the West Africa route, and then as a locum GP back home in Ayrshire, he took up a scientific research scholarship with Professor E. P. Cathcart at Glasgow University. One year into his new post, in 1913, Boyd Orr was informed that his mentor had accepted an invitation to become head of research in animal nutrition in a joint initiative being established by Aberdeen University and the North of Scotland College of Agriculture. Cathcart reversed his decision shortly afterwards, in order take up a professorship in London, but he recommended his thirty-three year old assistant for the vacancy in Aberdeen. With some reluctance, Boyd Orr applied for the post, and, in spite of his lack of experience, was appointed. In his autobiography, he admitted that the main attraction of the new job was the generous salary, which would allow him to marry his 'boyhood sweetheart', Elizabeth ('Bess') Callum. On his arrival in Aberdeen in April 1914, however, he was dismayed to discover only a research plan, but no building or laboratory for the new Nutrition Institute. He spent a feverish few months designing the buildings and laboratories and negotiating with the university and college authorities in order to secure finances for their construction. However, war broke out before serious building work could begin.

During his long tenure at the Rowett, Boyd Orr's contributions to public policy were both direct and indirect—some of his work, or the work of those around him, undoubtedly contributed to specific government measures, while, in a broader sense, his proselytising and campaigning helped shape official opinion in key areas. Recognition of his work saw Boyd Orr elected as a Fellow of the Royal Society in 1932, and knighted in 1935.

Especially worthy of note in this period was the research of David Lubbock (initially a volunteer at the Rowett, later Boyd Orr's son-in-law) on the positive impact of daily milk for schoolchildren in urban Scotland and Northern Ireland, and Boyd Orr's lobbying of Tom Johnston (Under-Secretary of State for Scotland in 1931) and Walter Elliot (Conservative MP with a medical and scientific background, first encountered by Boyd Orr in 1908 and thereafter a consistent supporter of his causes in Parliament and the Cabinet), which led to the expansion of research on health-nutrition links in Lanarkshire, and the Private Member's Bill allowing Scottish local authorities to provide cheap or free milk to all schoolchildren.

The origins of *Food, Health and Income* (1936),[172] the publication with which his name will forever be associated, can be traced back to Boyd Orr's experiences with the destitute during his student days in Glasgow, but more directly, it stemmed from his work on the Milk Marketing Board's reorganization committee, and the story of this publication reveals much about the balance Boyd Orr tried to strike between idealism and pragmatism, and his occasional impatience with politics and bureaucracy. His argument, based on the earlier work

---

172 Sir John Orr, Food, Health and Income. *Report on a survey of adequacy of diet in relation to income* (London: Macmillan, 1936). Note that the 'Boyd' element of his name did not invariably appear in Boyd Orr's publications, especially during the period before 1945.

in the Rowett, that the nation's milk production plans should benefit the health of the poor as well as the finances of the producers, did not go down well on a committee dominated by agricultural interests, but the new policy which eventually emerged, allowed for the expansion of the scheme to provide free milk to schoolchildren. Emboldened by this success, he used the Chadwick lecture in 1934 ('The National Food Supply and its Influence on Public Health')[173] to criticise the system of Agricultural Marketing Boards and recommend a 'comprehensive food and agriculture policy based on human needs'. The tone and content of this lecture led to calls from some officials and politicians for the withdrawal of government grants to the Rowett (an experience which led to a more cautious, pragmatic approach by Boyd Orr in later years), but Boyd Orr's friend Walter Elliot, by now a minister, successfully resisted this. Instead, Elliot showed his support for Boyd Orr and the Rowett by proposing that the data produced by the various dietary surveys carried out over the past few years should be collated and used as the basis for policy change.[174]

As he worked on the material, Boyd Orr launched into a publicity campaign of speeches, newspaper articles and radio broadcasts, in which he argued for a new food policy based on the health needs of the population. This alienated some senior civil servants, as well as the Minister of Health, Kingsley Wood, and led to the officials who had been working with Boyd Orr to request that their names should be removed from the report. It was clear that the government would not officially publish the document. Undeterred, Boyd Orr secured the support of Harold Macmillan, then the distinctly left-leaning Conservative M.P. for Stockton,

173 See Boyd Orr, *As I Recall*, p.113.
174 Cf. ibid, pp.113–115.

and *Food, Health and Income* was published in book form by Macmillan's family firm in 1936. Although the report was criticised in some quarters due to the limited nature of the sample, and the assumptions which underpinned its statements about nutritional needs, the key finding, that 'a diet completely adequate for health according to modern standards is reached only at an income level above that of fifty percent of the population', created political shock-waves, and established a strong case for government intervention.175

Whitehall scepticism and inertia ensured that there was little progress towards the development of a new food policy until the outbreak of war, although, as Christopher Harvie points out in *No Gods and Precious Few Heroes* (1998), his history of twentieth-century Scotland, Boyd Orr's findings provided background evidence which supported the expansion of unemployment assistance and 'special area' status for deprived regions throughout the UK.176

Wartime

Boyd Orr's work took on a fresh significance after 1939. While continuing his directorship at the Rowett, he co-authored (with David Lubbock) *Feeding the People in War-Time* (1940),177 joined the Cabinet Food Committee, played a significant part in influencing Lord Woolton, the Minister for Food, and wrote an astonishing number of papers and reports, including a study of infant mortality in Scotland in 1943. His book of 1942, *Fighting For What?* was effectively a manifesto for wide-ranging socio-economic change, encompassing diet and nutrition, housing, employment, and government (he writes of the importance of

175 Cf. ibid, Chapter 13.
176 Christopher Harvie, *No Gods and Precious Few Heroes: Twentieth Century Scotland* (London: Blackwell, 1998) pp.50–51; 72–73. Christopher Harvie, No Gods and Precious Few Heroes: Twentieth Century Scotland (London: Blackwell, 1998) pp.50–51; 72–73.
177 Sir John Orr and David M. Lubbock, *Feeding the People in War-Time* (London: Macmillan, 1940).

post-war 'world government').[178] Interestingly, the religious influences set out in Professor McFarland's paper can be seen in the book's dedication, with its passage of scripture, to the memory of Boyd Orr's son Billy, who was killed in the war. Perhaps Boyd Orr's slightly ambiguous position on religious matters is best illustrated through the correspondence he had with the editor of the Quaker journal *The Friend* in 1945, when the latter describes Boyd Orr's article for the journal as 'advocating what is sometimes called the Social Gospel'.[179]

The National Library of Scotland holds over one hundred wartime typescripts and manuscripts of Boyd Orr's articles, speeches, broadcast talks and reviews. In the longer term, his work became a vital part of the mosaic of data and reports which shaped the political determination that there should be no return to the social conditions of the 1930s, and established the case for the creation of the post-war welfare state.

Post-War Period

The foundations for Boyd Orr's post-war contributions, when he truly became the 'global citizen' of this publication's theme, were laid during the 30s and early 40s in the course of his extensive foreign visits on behalf of the Rowett, which had established his reputation in many quarters. In the United States in 1942, he met several members of the Roosevelt administration, and canvassed support for his ideas for post-war international coordination of food and agricultural policies. The U.S. government expected Boyd Orr to be part of the British delegation to the following year's Hot Springs Conference, designed to give effect to F. D.

---

178 Sir John Orr, *Fighting For What?* (London: Macmillan, 1942)
179 Papers of Lord Boyd Orr, CH, FRS, National Library of Scotland, Manuscripts Division, Acc.6545 [hereafter LBO], Box 1, Item 110, papers for an article for *The Friend* (1945), on post-war cooperation between nations.

Roosevelt's 'Freedom from Want', but, revealingly, Whitehall refused to send this 'unorthodox' figure. Following some lobbying, he was at the Quebec Conference in 1945, at which the Food and Agriculture Organization (FAO) of the UN was launched, with Boyd Orr as its first director-general.[180] At this point, he relinquished the seat in the Commons he had held for only a few months as an Independent MP for the Scottish Universities.

His time at the FAO, between 1945 and 1948, saw the organization formally established, but Boyd Orr became increasingly frustrated by its lack of power and the lack of interest shown by some governments (including his own) in its work. Although he became an effective and high-profile advocate for the FAO, he struggled to gain administrative control of the new organization. His major objective was to create international cooperation in order to increase agricultural production, particularly in the third world, while preventing price fluctuations and the accumulation of wasteful surpluses. In order to achieve this, he proposed the establishment of a World Food Board, with sweeping executive powers. The UN, heavily influenced by Britain and the United States, refused to sanction this, favouring only an advisory body, the World Food Council. Consequently, Boyd Orr announced his resignation, remaining in post only until his successor could be appointed.[181] He re-established his parliamentary connection by accepting a peerage in 1948, becoming Baron Boyd Orr of Brechin Mearns.

---

180 See Boyd Orr, *As I Recall*, Chapters 14 and 17.
181 Cf. ibid., Chpt. 18.

Boyd Orr's Nobel Prize, awarded in 1949, was in the 'Peace' rather than the 'Science' category. In his presentation speech, Gunnnar Jahn, chairman of the Nobel Committee, noted Boyd Orr's 'scientific contributions', but went on to say that 'they alone would not have earned him the Peace Prize, for scientific discoveries cannot, in themselves, create peace.' Instead, he argued, it is the use of science to 'promote cooperation between nations' that creates the value in relation to peace, and he linked this to Boyd Orr's international work (on the League of Nations committee of nutritional physiologists, at the FAO, and on the National Peace Council, the World Union of Peace Organisations, and the World Movement for World Federal Government).[182] In his short acceptance speech for the Peace Prize in December 1949,[183] and, in more depth, during his Nobel Lecture two days later,[184] Boyd Orr set out his thoughts on the linkages between science and technology, the economics of health and food, international cooperation, and the United Nations as a force for peace. The brief audio extract from the Lecture on the Nobel Prize Organisation website provides an opportunity to hear Boyd Orr's distinctive Ayrshire tones.[185]

He also served, successively, as Rector and Chancellor of the University of Glasgow, boosted his income in retirement by taking a number of business directorships, dabbled on the fringes of the movement for Scottish home rule, and lobbied continuously for policies to end poverty and malnutrition, and to promote world peace and world government. In the Lords he made occasional, telling,

182 Gunnar Jahn, 'The Nobel Peace Prize 1949, Presentation Speech by the Chairman of the Nobel Committee', <www.nobelprize.org/peace/laureates/1949/press.html>, accessed July 2013.
183 Lord Boyd Orr, 'Acceptance Speech on the Occasion of the Award of the Nobel Peace Prize in Oslo, December 10, 1949', <www.nobelprize.org/peace/laureates/1949/orr-acceptance.html>, accessed July 2013.
184 Lord Boyd Orr, 'Nobel Lecture, December 12, 1949', <www.nobelprize.org/peace/laureates/1949/orr-lecture.html>, accessed July 2013.
185 Audio link is at < http://www.nobelprize.org/mediaplayer/index.php?id=1339>, accessed July 2013.

interventions in debates on matters relating to food policy. He continued to campaign and write throughout his retirement, and was active up until his death in 1971.

Complexities and Contradictions

At one level, Boyd Orr appeared to be a man of unswerving moral certainties, with his compass clearly set. On closer examination, however, behind this facade, it is clear that there were serious complexities and contradictions in his make-up. As the man moulded by his Ayrshire roots made his way in the world, the light and shade emerged in his character, and the compromises involved in striking a balance between idealism and pragmatism came into play. Let us identify a few illustrative examples of this.

Boyd Orr was a man of science, yet his approach to scientific methodology was distinctly idiosyncratic. In later life, he acknowledged that the foundations for his scientific work were laid in the Glasgow University classes of Noel Paton, professor of Physiology, Samson Gemmell, professor of Clinical Medicine, and Sir William MacEwan, professor of Surgery. However, his claim that Paton taught him to write scientific papers by starting with the conclusions and then directing all the facts and arguments accordingly, scarcely seems a model of deductive reasoning, and perhaps casts an interesting light on some of Boyd Orr's subsequent publications![186]

186 See Boyd Orr, *As I Recall*, p.49.

While it would be going too far to say that for Boyd Orr the ends justified the means, there is some evidence to suggest that he could view his colleagues in a fairly instrumental way. Following his death, the journal *Nutrition Abstracts and Reviews* published a series of tributes in January 1972, one of which was written by Isabella Leitch, formerly of the Commonwealth Bureau of Animal Nutrition, and a colleague of Boyd Orr. Her comments were slightly ambiguous: 'A man full of contradictions, intensely ambitious but lacking the vanity that so often spurs ambition; always fair and loyal to his staff but interested in them primarily as the instruments that extended his own capacity to think and to translate thought into action.'[187]

The complexities, contradictions and ambiguities of Boyd Orr's character can perhaps best be illustrated with reference to his attitude towards government. He had an abiding faith in the power of governments to do good, and he fully understood that the impacts on public health provision that he sought were attainable only through concerted intervention, usually against the interests of markets and business. In order to achieve his ends, he was aware of the need to strike the right balance between idealism and pragmatism, on occasion openly defying the prevailing Whitehall orthodoxies (as when he secured independent publication of *Food, Health and Income*), but on other occasions showing a willingness to 'play the game' by conciliating, or avoiding antagonizing those in positions of power and authority. Boyd Orr's papers provide numerous examples of this. For example, when Lord Astor, the proprietor of *The Observer*, asked him in April 1945 to write an article setting out his criticism of government policy on

---

187 LBO, Box 2, Isabella Leitch, 'Tribute to Lord Boyd Orr', in *Nutrition Abstracts and Reviews*, Vol. 42 (Jan. 1972). For a detailed analysis of Boyd Orr's team management approaches at the Rowett, see David Smith, 'The Use of "Team Work" in the Practical Management of Research in the Inter-War Period: John Boyd Orr at the Rowett Research Institute', *Minerva*, Vol. 37 (1999), pp 259–80.

wheat imports, Boyd Orr declined, noting in a letter to Astor that while he saw the policy as seriously deficient, he would not criticize it publicly because that 'would raise hostility at the Ministry of Agriculture'.188 Perhaps he was extra-sensitive about these matters, not just due to the pre-war threats to the Rowett's funding, but also because it seems that his criticism of food policy had been seized upon by the enemy earlier in the war. In 1941, he wrote to a BBC Talks Assistant urging caution regarding the content of a forthcoming broadcast: 'If we make out the food position to be rather serious, as in my opinion it is, we will be handing ammunition to Haw-Haw who, to my intense annoyance, is already continually quoting me or rather mis-quoting me.'189 Nonetheless, he prized individual freedoms and was suspicious of the effect of government policy on scientists. There are numerous examples of this in his papers, with his faith in the virtue of centralized planning balanced by, as he wrote in a letter to the publishers Macmillan in 1940, a strong belief in 'freedom of thought and expression' and warnings about the dangers of 'scientists being muzzled'.190

Despite his proximity to the corridors of power, he was uncomfortable in office, turning down at least one offer of appointment before the Second World War (in 1937 he had refused the position of Chief Medical Officer in the Scottish Department of Health, apparently concerned that this would restrict his freedom to campaign for a new food policy),191 and ultimately finding the director-generalship of the FAO quite uncongenial. On these occasions, it would seem that his idealism trumped his pragmatism.

---

188 LBO, Box 1, Item 101, Boyd Orr's correspondence with Lord Astor, April 1945.
189 LBO, Box 1, Item 48, Boyd Orr's letter to Miss Christine Orr, BBC Talks Assistant, 22 Mar. 1941.
190 LBO, Box 1, Item 41, Boyd Orr's letter to Macmillan publishers accompanying Dec. 1940 book review.
191 According to a 'Biographical Note' ('passed by the British Censor 17 Apr. 1944') 'for overseas use only'. LBO, Box 1.

Despite his faith in the power of government, he held idiosyncratic views about leadership. His papers contain two pages of undated notes (probably written in 1945) on the question 'Should we educate for leadership?' He opposed the idea, instead favouring education 'for intelligent citizenship', citing the example of Germany as a case of 'too much leadership and too little thinking by the population', and noting that the 'great leaders of the world' are produced by experience rather than specialised education: 'Joe Stalin never attended any school like Eton or Harrow, not did Keir Hardy [sic]... or Lloyd George.'[192] In Boyd Orr's view, training for leadership should be practical, with those ambitious to be Health Ministers 'made to live in the slums for a while' and would-be coal industry bosses 'put down the pits for a couple of years'.[193]

Boyd Orr's personal politics were complex. His pragmatic approach led him to work effectively across the party political divides, prizing his good working relations with characters as diverse as Maxton and Churchill, and, of course, his influence during the 1930s was mediated by senior Conservatives like Walter Elliot and Harold Macmillan. He was elected as an Independent MP in 1945, and subsequently sat on the cross benches in the House of Lords. While he was happy to work with avowedly partisan groups from time to time (his papers contain scripts for speeches to, for example, the Socialist Teachers meeting in Glasgow in 1944),[194] he was wary of becoming too closely identified with them, fearing a negative impact on his broader work. For example, in March 1940, having given a talk at the Fabian Society—and been reimbursed to the tune of four guineas

192 LBO, Box 1, Item 107, Boyd Orr's notes on 'Should We Educate for Leadership?', undated but probably 1945.
193 Ibid.
194 LBO, Box 1, Item 100, Boyd Orr's 'Summary of Address to Socialist Teachers Meeting, Glasgow, 1944'.

(Boyd Orr: 'which is rather less than a third-class ticket')—he declined an invitation from the General Secretary to join the Society. As he wrote: 'it would be unwise in my present position to join any society which has a political flavour. If I were not in my present job, I should certainly join the Society.'[195] In lieu of membership, he made a contribution of £1 towards the Fabians' 'excellent research and publication activities'.[196]

His business interests and directorships also brought him into close proximity with those on the right of the political spectrum. In May 1944 he wrote a 'Confidential Note' at the request of the Vice-Chairman of the Midland Bank, headed 'The Swing to the Left'. In fact, this document recommended that those (like the Vice-Chairman) who were worried about the possible rise of 'the left' should understand the reasons behind this, and 'they may then be able to direct the forces along safe lines'. For Boyd Orr, this would involve serious state planning and delivery of promises made to the people.[197]

In later life, he maintained his stance of being the sympathetic, yet guarded, associate of leftist causes. He served as President of Medical Aid for Vietnam and contributed to the Scotland-USSR Friendship Society, in addition to his role as President of the National Peace Council, the World Union of Peace Organisations, and the Movement for World Federal Government.

195 LBO, Boyd Orr's letter to John Parker, MP, General Secretary of the Fabian Society, 22 Mar. 1940.
196 Ibid.
197 LBO, Box 1, Item 93, Boyd Orr's note on 'The Swing to the Left', 11 May 1944, a 'confidential note written at the request of Mr Sadd' who was Vice-Chairman of the Midland Bank Limited.

His papers contain correspondence with Vanessa Redgrave giving permission for his name to be included in an anti-Vietnam War petition sent to *The Times*,[198] and a personal invitation from Barbara Castle to be part of the leading group in the Anti-Apartheid march of November 1963 (he was too ill to attend but sent a handwritten message of support to Castle).[199] The papers also contain evidence of his scepticism regarding some of the activities of the luminaries of the left. In correspondence with Bertrand Russell in the summer of 1964, Boyd Orr reluctantly agreed to join Russell's British 'Who Killed Kennedy?' Committee, while making it clear that he felt this was 'not likely to be useful' and would be a distraction from the disarmament campaigns.[200]

Boyd Orr's nationalism was instinctive, although, again, his suspicion of parties meant that he retained a healthy scepticism towards its creed. No one reading his personal papers can be in any doubt that he was a proud, if self-reflective, Scot. He received regular invitations from around the globe, along the lines of his 'Talk by an Ayrshire Man' in 1942 to the Canada Club in New York, on the theme of 'What Scotsmen in America might do to help their native land'.[201] A set of notes on 'If I Were Minister of Food' contains four pages of ideas for massive government intervention, and a series of 'questions for discussion which included: 'Is the cooking of Scotland really worse than that of other countries?' He suspected that the answer would be in the affirmative: 'If it is worse, is it due

---

198 LBO, Box 2, 'Correspondence', Boyd Orr's letter to Vanessa Redgrave.
199 LBO, Box 2 , 'Correspondence', Boyd Orr's correspondence with Barbara Castle MP, Honorary President of the Anti-Apartheid Movement (Castle's letter 14 Oct. 1963, Boyd Orr's note of reply undated).
200 LBO, Box 2 , 'Correspondence', Boyd Orr's correspondence with Bertrand Russell (the Earl Russell), May and July 1964.
201 LBO, Box 1, Item 65, Boyd Orr's script for 'A Talk by an Ayrshire Man' to the Canada Club, New York on topic of 'What Scotsmen in America Might Do to Help Their Native Land', 2 Dec. 1942.

mainly to ignorance or to lack of proper cooking facilities?'[202] He pursued the themes further in a 1944 talk on 'Scots Food for Scots People', in which he recommended that school meals should 'consist mainly of ... Scottish foods', prepared by 'the bigger girls'.[203]

There could be apparent contradictions between Boyd Orr's nationalism and his international outlook. His proselytising for 'world government' could be countered by a more narrow focus. In 1940 he wrote (by invitation) for the *Scots Independent*: 'There is a lot of nonsense talked about Internationalism. If we cannot put our own country in order, how can we put the whole world in order. [*sic*]'[204] Perhaps this was a case of giving his audience what it wanted to hear?

Conclusion

In conclusion, as Professor McFarland's paper makes clear, it is important for us to avoid the trap of viewing Boyd Orr 'through the prism of present-day values and concerns'. However, on the other hand, it is equally important for us to recognise his prescience, and acknowledge the fact that, in so many ways, we share his preoccupations and concerns, on such matters as public health and social exclusion, diet and nutrition, the role of the United Nations, and third-world poverty. Some would perhaps question the current relevance of Boyd Orr, a product of a bygone era of dirigisme, and a man with an abiding faith in the power of governments to do good. However, his life and work contains relevant lessons for us still. Scientific and policy studies continue to show the significance of the

202 LBO, Box 1, Item 83, Boyd Orr's script for an unspecified purpose (address? talk? article?), undated, but probably 1944 on topic of 'If I Were Minister of Food'.
203 LBO, Box 1, Item 94, Boyd Orr's script for a talk in Edinburgh on 'Scots Food for Scots People', 1944.
204 LBO, Box 1, Item 42, Boyd Orr's 'New Year Message for 1941', written in Dec. 1940 for the *Scots Independent*, which had commissioned statements from prominent Scots.

links between income, diet, and health, and the persistent prevalence of poverty in the midst of affluence. Governments in the UK and beyond struggle to deal with fresh variants of the issues which inspired *Food, Health and Income*, Boyd Orr's vision for the FAO remains unfulfilled, and fundamental questions continue to arise about the role of the UN in the quest for international peace and stability. Boyd Orr's concerns and preoccupations are also ours.

Beyond all of this, with his undoubted flaws, foibles and contradictions, his combination of pragmatism and idealism, his preparedness to work constructively with people from different parts of the political spectrum in the interest of progressive policies, Boyd Orr was, despite the Victorian demeanour, a rather modern man in so many respects!

6

'I wonder why it is that they make such a fuss of me?': Alexander Fleming in Historical Context

Kevin Brown

Alexander Fleming always felt uncomfortable when being awarded an honorary degree, the freedom of a city, or indeed any honour. Showing true Scottish generosity rather than stereotypical parsimony, he wished to give something back on such occasions, and, realising that the honour was for the discovery of penicillin as much as it was for the discoverer, decided that the most appreciated gift of all would be a piece of 'the mould that made penicillin'. Samples of *Penicillium notatum* were grown and fixed on absorbent paper and mounted between two blank spectacle lenses. These mould medallions were then given as gifts. When the actress Marlene Dietrich, who had something of a crush on Fleming, invited him to dinner, he ended the evening by putting his hand in his pocket and pulling out one of these mould medallions. Other recipients included Queen Elizabeth the Queen Mother, the Duke of Edinburgh, Pope Pius XII, Winston Churchill, and Franklin D. Roosevelt. Edgar Lawley, the Chairman of the Board of Governors of St Mary's Hospital where Fleming worked for most of his life, had his mould medallion mounted in a gold surround almost like a medieval saint's reliquary.[205]

---

205 K. Brown and D. Eveleigh, 'Preservation of Fungal Herbarium Cultures: The Sale of an Alexander Fleming *Penicillium notatum* Preserved Medallion', *Society for Industrial Mycology News*, 47/3 (1997), pp.116–18.

Fleming himself was greeted with adulation wherever he went throughout the world. In 1948 in Barcelona, the toreadors, grateful for the use of penicillin to treat their infected wounds from the bullrings, knelt before him as a mark of homage. In many ways he was treated as the Princess Diana of his day, though he felt that his admirers had the 'impression that I was Winston or Princess Elizabeth' and felt uncomfortable with all the attention.[206] When he died the modest doctor from Ayrshire had his ashes interred in the crypt of St Paul's Cathedral as a national hero. Yet he himself wondered 'why it is that they make such a fuss of me?'[207]

The simple answer to Fleming's question was implicit in the mould medallions that Fleming gave away so freely. Fleming was fêted as the man who had discovered penicillin and kick-started the antibiotic revolution in medicine. If a mould medallion can go for auction at bids in the region of £25,000, how much is penicillin itself worth? When its impact in saving countless lives and improving the quality of others is born in mind, it is priceless. It had been hailed as a wonder drug and as a miracle cure in the Second World War when it had first come to public attention. It was widely reported that as a result of penicillin, as well as of other medical advances such as blood transfusion that came out of the Second World War, a soldier's chance of dying as a result of war wounds was only one in one hundred, a third of the death rate from wounds in the First World War.[208] The wartime press had built up interest in penicillin as good news in the midst of depressing war news and had lauded it as an example of British achievement. Although Fleming was not the only person concerned in the

---

206 British Library [hereafter BL], Add MS 56191, Fleming's Diary, 27 May 1948.
207 BL, Add MS 5615, John Cameron, 1956.
208 M. Clodfelter, *Warfare and Armed Conflicts: A Statistical Reference to Casualty and Other Figures*, 1618–1991 (Jefferson, NC: McFarland, 1992), pp.262–3.

development of penicillin, his role was stressed by the press, partly because he was prepared to speak to the journalists but also because his role was more understandable to the layman than that of dull laboratory work, though he had done plenty of that too. There is something romantic in the story of the humble doctor who one day notices that by chance a spore of mould has contaminated the Petri dish of bacteria that he was studying and has dissolved the bacteria. That chance observation then leads the way to the development of a lifesaving drug. Fleming's story could also be depicted, albeit inaccurately, as the classic story of rags to riches, from a humble upbringing on an Ayrshire hill farm to a last resting place in a pantheon of national heroes.

Fleming, though, belonged to the entire world by the time of his death. He was mourned as far afield as the Dominican Republic where flags were lowered in a national gesture of respect. His remains in St Paul's are covered by a slab of Pentelic marble from the quarries from which the stone for building the Parthenon in Athens was hewn. He had been fêted in Greece as much as he had been all over the world, and his second wife was Greek. The stone bears two symbols: the thistle, marking his pride in his Scottish birth, and the fleur-de-lis, the emblem of St Mary's Hospital in London which had been the scene of his labours for fifty-three years.[209] Although he had moved to London in 1895 at the age of fourteen, after less than a year at Kilmarnock Academy, he always remained conscious and proud of his Scottish roots, serving as a private in the London Scottish Regiment in his spare time and becoming an active member of the London Ayrshire Society.

209 K. Brown, *Penicillin Man: Alexander Fleming and the Antibiotic Revolution* (Stroud: Sutton, 2004), p.202.

He also firmly believed that his upbringing at Lochfield Farm near Darvel had encouraged him to develop a keen interest in natural history and honed his acute powers of observation that were later to enable him to see some significance in the chance observation of a chance contaminant on a culture plate.

Certainly, Fleming had an eye for the quirky and for the unusual, as well as a way of looking beyond the obvious, which may have come from his boyhood surrounded by nature at Lochfield. He later claimed that 'my powers of observation were sharpened by my search for pewits' [*sic*] eggs in the fields and moors, my patience increased by the guddling for trout in the Glen Water' and that 'you picked up many interesting things about wild nature that you might not have learned at school.'[210] He also cultivated inventiveness in developing new games and an ingenuity that was to be his hallmark as a scientist. This playful side of things is revealed by Fleming's interest in art where, instead of using oils or watercolours to paint a picture, he used differently pigmented bacteria to produce what he called germ paintings. They may have been a bit of fun, mere painting by numbers with bugs, but to do them at all, let alone do them well, demanded great expertise and knowledge, as well as being the fruit of the imaginativeness and receptiveness to something that did not fit into a preconceived pattern first shown at Lochfield.[211]

Fleming's time at Kilmarnock Academy was short and it was unremarkable. He was enrolled on 28 August 1894 and moved to London in the summer of 1895 to live with his older brother Tom, an oculist, and to continue his education at the Regent Street Polytechnic.[212] Fleming, with a good memory and an innate ability

210 L. J. Ludovici, *Alexander Fleming, Discoverer of Penicillin* (London: Dakers,1952), pp.22–4.
211 BL, Add MS 56217, H.J. Bunker, n.d.
212 Burns Monument Centre, East Ayrshire Archive, Kilmarnock Academy Admissions Register, 28 August 1894; Robert Fleming, *Sir Alexander Fleming, a Personal Story of his Life* (privately published, 1958), p. 22.

to get to the heart of a subject, showed no signs to his school fellows of putting much effort into his studies at the Academy though he was ahead of his contemporaries by about a year as he had been at his previous school in Darvel. Although Kilmarnock Academy was considered advanced in teaching science at all, thanks to the personal initiative of the rector Dr Hugh Dickie, its teaching of physics, chemistry and biology was basic and probably of little value to the future scientist.[213] Indeed, when he finished his education at the age of sixteen Fleming seemed destined for a business career and began work as a shipping clerk, a job he hated and for which he was unsuited. Only a legacy from an uncle and a scholarship which he himself won after success in a competitive examination to study medicine at St Mary's Hospital Medical School allowed him to leave the detested commercial world and become a medical student in 1901.[214]

It was at St Mary's Hospital, Paddington, that Fleming was to carry out the work with which he made his mark on medicine. Entering as a student in October 1901, he was to remain there until his death in March 1955. Like Kilmarnock Academy, St Mary's can lay claim to two Nobel laureates on its staff, the first being Fleming who received the 1945 prize for medicine for his discovery of penicillin at the hospital, and the other being Rodney Porter, a laureate in 1972, for his work at St Mary's on the structure and functions of the immunoglobulins. It was at St Mary's that Fleming came under the influence of the charismatic and controversial immunologist Sir Almroth Wright, founder of the Inoculation Department, a semi-autonomous research institute at St Mary's. Nicknamed 'Sir Almost Right' and 'Sir Always Wrong' by his many enemies in the medical

---

213 BL Add MS 56215, Agnes Smith; BL Add MS 56218, Hamilton Dunnett., n.d.
214 Imperial College Healthcare NHS Trust Archives, St Mary's Hospital, Paddington, MS/AD20/2, Roll of Sudents, October 1901.

profession of whom he was ultra-critical, Wright was to be immortalised by his friend George Bernard Shaw in his play *The Doctor's Dilemma* (1906), a drama still topical today with its theme of how to decide which patients to treat if there are too many people in need of treatment and too few resources. Wright was also to become a hate figure to the suffragette movement on account of his trenchant statements that women were medically unfit to have the vote, though his friend Shaw was hardly more sensitive with his rebuttal of Wright's position to the effect that he admitted that women did not share the great intelligence of Wright and himself, but that as neither did most men, there was no reason to deny women the vote on grounds of lack of intelligence. Wright was not only capable of provoking intense loathing, he was also able to enthuse and inspire a generation of young doctors with his ideas, foremost among them Alexander Fleming.[215]

Although his greatest achievement was the development of the first effective anti-typhoid vaccine which was to be a life saver in the First World War, Wright had ambitions to establish a new form of treatment, which he called vaccine therapy, as the way forward in medicine. Wright's vaccine therapy was the use of vaccines to treat disease by stimulating the body's own immune system to fight against an existing infection, and was based on Eli Metchnikov's understanding of the role of the phagocytes in fighting infection. Wright was in touch with most of the leading European bacteriologists and immunologists of his day, some of whom like Metchnikov and Robert Koch actually visited St Mary's to see for themselves what he was doing. Fleming acknowledged Metchnikov's importance by hanging a signed photograph of Metchnikov in his laboratory, a visual symbol

---

215 See M. Dunnill, *The Plato of Praed Street: The Life and Times of Almroth Wright* (London: Royal Society of Medicine, 2000).

of the chains of inspiration in science. Indeed, bacteriology was an exciting new science which seemed to point the way ahead for great advances in the treatment of infections when Fleming was a young man. He had been born in the year in which his fellow Scot, Alexander Ogston, had described the bacterium staphylococcus, which was to play a part in Fleming's discovery, and with which Louis Pasteur had successfully immunized sheep against anthrax; later Fleming remarked that 'for Pasteur, 1881 was a memorable year; so it was for me, for it was then that I was born'.[216]

The development of bacteriology had enabled scientists to identify the causes of infection more precisely and develop diagnostic tests. However, there was less of an advance in ways of treating disease. Immunology seemed to be one way forward and chemotherapy another. However, the first modern chemotherapeutic agent was salvarsan developed by Wright's friend Paul Ehrlich, an arsenical compound for the targeted treatment of syphilis against which mercury had hitherto been the most effective treatment. Ehrlich had sent an early sample of salvarsan, otherwise known as 'compound 606', to Wright, but, having no sympathy for chemotherapy in any form, the immunologist had passed it on to his junior, Alexander Fleming. More open-minded than the chief to whom he always remained loyal, Fleming was able to build up a reputation as a pox doctor because of the success with which he was able to administer salvarsan, safely and relatively painlessly, through the then new technique of intravenous injection.[217] Among Fleming's patients were fellow other-rankers in the London Scottish Regiment. Fleming was in turn to be caricatured by his artist friend Ronald Gray

216 A. Fleming, 'Louis Pasteur', *British Medical Journal*, 1 (1947), p.517.
217 A. Fleming, and L.Colebrook, 'On the Use of Salvarsan in the Treatment of Syphilis', *Lancet*, 1 (1911), pp.1631–4.

as 'Private 606' in his London Scottish uniform with its hodden grey kilt, the inevitable cigarette in his mouth and with a syringe in place of his bayonet and dirk (Fig. 5).[218]

Figure 5. 'Private 606' by Ronald Gray, an artist friend of Fleming, showing Fleming in 1911 in the uniform of the London Scottish Regiment, with, in place of a rifle and fixed bayonet, an outsized syringe for administering salvarsan, known as 'compound 606'. Salvarsan, which Fleming administered successfully through the new technique of intravenous injection, was used in the treatment of syphilis.
Used by permission of the Alexander Fleming Laboratory Museum.

218 Ronald Gray, *Private 606*, 1936, now at the Basic Medical Research Centre Alexander Fleming, Vari, Greece.

It was not with the London Scottish Regiment that Fleming was to see service during the First World War but with the Royal Army Medical Corps as part of a team headed by Sir Almroth Wright studying the bacteriology of wound infections at a military hospital set up in the Casino at Boulogne. There, using his ingenuity and practical glass-blowing skills to construct an artificial wound, Fleming was able to demonstrate that the use of strong antiseptics on wounds was doing more harm than good, and by the end of the war was an acknowledged expert on wound infections, which would have entitled him to be considered more than a footnote in the history of bacteriology.[219] However, at the end of the war, he returned to St Mary's and was to make a discovery which in many ways could be considered the precursor of penicillin, the enzyme lysozyme.

In November 1921, Fleming had a cold and a drop of nasal mucus fell on to a plate of bacteria. Ever ready to break the rules in pursuit of an interesting outcome, he wondered what would happen if he mixed it in with the bacteria and after a few weeks found signs of lysis, of something within the mucus that was dissolving the bacteria. That enzyme which he named lysozyme (i.e. an enzyme which dissolves), was present in many other body fluids, including saliva and tears.[220] Human tears were a good source of lysozyme and for a time visitors to Fleming's laboratory would be pounced upon to have lemon juice squeezed into their eyes to produce 'tear antiseptic'. Not surprisingly visitors soon got wise to that and Fleming found that he had to pay his laboratory technicians to allow him to squeeze lemon juice into their eyes to make them cry. In those days the

219 A. E. Wright and A. Fleming, 'The Aerobic Infections of War Wounds', *Medical Research Council Special Report Series*, no. 39 (1919), pp.70–8.
220 A. Fleming, 'On a Remarkable Bacteriolytic Element found in Tissues and Secretions', *Proceedings of the Royal Society*, B, 93 (1922), pp.252–60.

laboratory technicians were known as 'lab boys', irrespective of their actual age. A cartoonist on *Punch* got hold of the story and assumed that the 'lab boys' must be schoolboys. The result was a marvellous image of schoolboys queuing up to be thrashed to produce tear antiseptic in return for a fee of one penny (Fig. 2).[221]

Fleming considered his best work as a scientist to have been done on lysozyme, an honest assessment by an honourable man, but the problem with it was that it did not act against the most harmful of bacteria. As he worked in a research institute where the hospital ward was seen as an extension of the laboratory and research was geared towards therapeutics, Fleming was later to be attracted to penicillin by its similarity in a culture plate to the action of lysozyme. The first reaction of other scientists to Fleming's findings was not as enthusiastic as he had hoped, mainly because he was a poor public speaker and was often inaudible. His reputation as someone interested in quirky little eccentricities also worked against him, as when he presented his work to the Medical Research Club, Sir Henry Dale later recalled that everyone had said, 'Oh, is that not charming, that is the sort of naturalist's observation which Fleming makes.'[222]

Fleming's next discovery, that of penicillin, was similarly to make little initial impact when first published in 1929. On 3 September 1928, he had returned to work after a holiday at his house in Suffolk to find that a Petri dish that he had left on his laboratory bench before going away had become contaminated by a fungus. Such contamination was an occupational hazard, especially in Fleming's cluttered, musty and somewhat dusty laboratory, and the mould aroused little

221 J. H. Dowd, *Punch*, 28 Jun. 1922. The original art work is now in the collections of the Alexander Fleming Laboratory Museum.
222 BL, Add MS 56219, H.H. Dale, n.d.

interest in him. What did interest him more was that there were no bacteria growing close to the mould. Something from the fungus obviously had inhibited the growth of the *Staphylococci*, a substance which Fleming at first called 'mould juice' and later named 'penicillin' after the fungus, *Penicillium notatum*, which had produced it. Ever the master of understatement, his initial comment was 'That's funny'. Before his holiday, he had been working on the bacterium *Staphylococcus aureus* for a chapter of a Medical Research Council textbook, *A System of Bacteriology* (1930). In the course of this work he had prepared some culture plates of *Staphylococci* in order to make some observations.[223] Leaving cultures lying around for a few weeks after he had finished with them and then checking them for anything interesting or unusual was Fleming's usual way of working for he was very much in the tradition of the nineteenth-century naturalist interested in unusual phenomena.

Fleming's great significance in the development of antibiotics is that he recognised that there was a clinical potential for the use of penicillin if the problems of stabilising and purifying it could be overcome. He was mainly thinking in terms of using it topically, on the surface of a wound, like a local antiseptic. In this he was fitting his discovery into the clinical ideas of the time, but more importantly, he anticipated its use as an antibiotic (although the word itself was not coined until 1941) when he wrote that 'it is suggested that it may be an efficient antiseptic for application to, or injection into, areas infected with penicillin-sensitive microbes' and suggested a systemic use for it by injection into the blood stream.[224]

223 A. Fleming, 'The Staphylococci' in Medical Research Council, *A System of Bacteriology in Relation to Medicine* (London: HMSO, 1929), pp.11–28.
224 A. Fleming, 'On the Antibacterial Action of Cultures of a Penicillium, with Special Reference to their Use in the Isolation of *B. Influenzae*,' British Journal of Experimental Pathology, 10 (1929), pp.226–36.

Although he suggested the possibilities for penicillin in 1929 and himself did further work on penicillin in 1934, it was not until 1939 that things were in place for a further advance to be made when a research team at the Sir William School of Pathology at the University of Oxford was attracted to penicillin as they were approaching the end of a project on the biochemistry of lysozyme, Fleming's earlier discovery, and were looking for a new research project. As the biochemist on that team, Ernst Chain, had an expertise in enzymes, he was attracted to penicillin for the same reason Fleming had been—its similarity to the action of lysozyme. The interest of the Oxford team was initially purely academic. Only as they progressed with their work did they become aware of the therapeutic value of stabilising and purifying penicillin, a contrast with the ethos of the Inoculation Department at St Mary's where clinical applications were ever at the forefront of the work being done.

Penicillin caught the imagination of a wartime public craving good news in the summer of 1942. Almroth Wright immediately wrote to *The Times* hailing Fleming as the discoverer after reading an editorial on penicillin which failed to mention the discoverer or indeed those who had developed it:

> You refrained from putting a laurel wreath for this discovery on anyone's brow… on the principle *palmam qui meruit ferat* [let he who merited the palm bear it] it should be decreed to Professor Alexander Fleming of this research laboratory. For he is the discoverer of penicillin and was the author also of the original suggestion that this substance might prove to have important applications in medicine.[225]

225 *The Times*, 27 August 1942.

Immediately, the Oxford team staked their claims to a share of the glory with Robert Robinson declaring that 'a laurel wreath, a bouquet at least, and a handsome one, should be presented to H. W. Florey'.[226] It laid down the battle lines to competing claims for the discovery of penicillin between Fleming and the Oxford team, with Florey becoming ever more paranoid that Fleming was stealing all the glory. It is a futile and sterile debate as there is surely enough glory to go round, and with enough to spare.

Whilst in the popular imagination, where the element of chance lends an aura of romance to Fleming's role compared with the hard slog of laboratory bench work at Oxford, Fleming is most remembered, the role of Florey and his team was undoubtedly recognised in the scientific community. Fleming, Florey and Chain shared the 1945 Nobel Prize for Medicine for the discovery and development of penicillin. Inevitably Fleming received the lion's share of the nominations, with twenty compared to thirteen for Florey and one for Chain.[227] Fleming received it for the discovery of penicillin and Florey and Chain for its development. This might seem fair enough. Yet, behind Florey and Chain was a larger multidisciplinary team; much of their success was down to that teamwork. Fleming fully acknowledged the role that the Oxford team had played when he wrote to Florey saying that 'although my work started you on the penicillin hunt, it was you who have made it a practical proposition and it is good that you should get the credit.'[228]

226 Ibid., 31 August 1942.
227 Nobel Archives. Karolinska Institute, Stockholm, register of nominations, 1945, entries for Fleming, Florey and Chain.
228 Royal Society, HF/1/3//2/12, letter from A. Fleming to H. Florey, 2 September 1942

Fleming's role in the story of penicillin had been one of making the original observation from which all else was to flow and of seeing the significance of something which others might have missed. His training as a medical doctor and bacteriologist, his own acute powers of observation and love of improvising, his open-mindedness and his previous work all made him receptive to the significance of what he had seen by chance. The potential in that observation was to be developed by people working as a team at a time when multidisciplinary teamwork was the way forward in medical research. He himself fitted in with the older tradition of the lone researcher and was inspired by the work of those who had gone before him in what was then still the new field of bacteriology at the outset of his career, a field in which he certainly made his own mark.

In the years following the end of the Second World War and the award of the Nobel Prize, Fleming received honours all over the world. He was in demand everywhere and took on a new role as an ambassador for both the United Kingdom and for Science. Cecil Weir, who had worked with him at the Ministry of Supply when Fleming was on the Penicillin Committee charged with getting production of the antibiotic underway in wartime, commented that 'it is very good for British science that this British discovery is being accorded such a well-deserved award, that your marvellous work is receiving such unstinted honour'.[229] However, Fleming, the modest if dour Scot from Ayrshire, was more than a representative of his country. He came to represent the kindly and human face of science at a time when, following the dropping of the atom bomb, science had come to seem frightening. People were tired of the larger-than-life figures of wartime and welcomed a man who could be Everyman but who had achieved great things.

Fleming himself failed to see what all the fuss was about. When elected a Fellow of the Royal Society in 1943, his friends and colleagues at St Mary's marked the occasion with the gift of a silver salver. In his thank-you speech Fleming misquoted the Ayrshire poet Robert Burns, with the words 'Would to God the giftie gie us / To see ourselves as others see us', yet he had misquoted it out of context, giving the impression that he was saying that no one had recognised his talents until quite late, but that was the opposite of what he intended. He actually meant to say that he did not think himself anything out of the ordinary.[230] His achievements, though, speak for themselves.

---

229 BL, Add MS 56114, letter from Cecil Weir to Alexander Fleming, 27 October 1945.
230 BL Add Ms 56114, Douglas MacLeod, n.d.